"North Star Ram"

RAMTHA

THE MIND GLADIATORS OF THE FUTURE

The Unusual Story
of How to Master Time,
Conquer One's Self,
and Reach Immortality

Hun Nal Ye PUBLISHING

THE MIND GLADIATORS OF THE FUTURE

For more information about Ramtha's teachings, contact:
Ramtha's School of Enlightenment
P.O. Box 1210, Yelm, WA, 98597 USA
www.ramtha.com

Book Cover Design, courtesy of
Paulina Amador of Holo-graphics.net
Book text illustrations, courtesy of Lizzie Guerrero
All Rights Reserved

ISBN # 978-0988-2983-78

Hun Nal Ye Publishing
Retracing the Footsteps of Ancient Wisdom in Our History
"North Star Ram"

P.O. Box 15232
Tumwater, Washington 98511, U.S.A.
www.Hun-Nal-Ye.com

*"The way you become immortal
is when you create immortality."*

— Ramtha

CONTENTS

PART 2
TO BECOME THE MASTER OF TIME, YOU MUST CONQUER THE BEAST

PART 3
FUTURE MIND AND THE GARDEN
OF FANTASTIC REALISM

AN IMPORTANT MESSAGE

This book is based on Ramtha Dialogues®, a series of audio recordings of lectures and teachings given by Ramtha. Ramtha has chosen American woman JZ Knight as his only channel to deliver his message. The only language he uses to communicate his teachings is the English language. His style of speech is very unique and uncommon, which is often misunderstood as archaic or odd. He has explained that his choice of words, his alteration of words, his sentence construction and arrangement of verbs and nouns, his breaks and pauses in midsentence, are all intentional to reach multiple layers of acceptance and interpretation present in an audience composed of people from a diversity of cultural backgrounds and walks of life.

In order to preserve the authenticity of the message given by Ramtha, we rendered the original words as they were spoken to allow the reader to experience the teaching as if they had been present. If you find some sentences that seem incorrect or odd according to the current linguistic form of your language, we encourage you to read that portion again, endeavoring to grasp the meaning behind the words rather than simply being critical of the literary construction. Our best wishes to you. Enjoy your reading.

ACKNOWLEDGMENTS

First of all, we would like to express our heartfelt gratitude to JZ Knight for making possible, through her person and her unwavering dedication, the channeling of Ramtha's teachings, the Lord of the Wind. We also want to thank her for giving us permission to create and publish this original work of Ramtha's teachings that we lovingly and proudly present to you in this book. Our most sincere thanks to our teacher Ramtha the Enlightened One, for his extraordinary and vast legacy of wisdom and love for humanity that he has continued to share with us without interruption for more than three decades already.

We would also like to thank everyone who helped and supported us in the production of this book you now hold in your hands: Lilia

Macías Leal, for her dedication, inspiration and support; Liliana Torres, for her diligence and efficiency; Pat Richker of JZK, Inc., for transcribing and proofreading the final edition; Special thanks and acknowledgment to Mexican artist, Lizzie Guerrero, for the interior book illustrations; Stephanie Millham, for her advice and help; Jaime Leal Anaya, for the creation and edition of this work, as well as the editorial design; and Paulina Amador of Holo-graphics.net, for putting together the thought-provoking new dust jacket design. We would also like to extend our sincere thanks to Rodrigo Vildosola and Julio Saavedra. We deeply value all their help and sincere friendship. Without them, and you, the reader, this book would not be now a reality.

Thank you all and Godspeed!

INTRODUCTION BY THE EDITOR

Prelude:
The Secret of Immortality

"All the younger Gods were for welcoming Psyche at once, and Hermes was sent to bring her hither. The maiden came, a shy newcomer among those bright creatures. She took the cup that Hebe held out to her, drank the divine ambrosia, and became immortal.

"Light came to her face like moonrise, two radiant wings sprang from her shoulders; and even as a butterfly bursts from its dull cocoon, so the human Psyche blossomed into immortality."[1]

Time is invisible and an abstract concept but it becomes something quite real when its cold thoroughfare sculpts a very visible trace on our face, and the body struggles, fatigued with age. The clarity and vitality that often escape us in the autumn of our life's journey brings us face to face with its elusive but real presence.

1   "The Trial of Psyche." *Old Greek Folk Stories Told Anew by Josephine P. Peabody.* Riverside Literature Series. Houghton Mifflin Co., Vol. 114. Cambridge, 1897.

During the times of the great Greek Epics — the stories of the Gods from Olympus and that culture's renowned thinkers and philosophers — the highest virtue a mortal person could strive for was being remembered. They hoped that their name and the conquests of their life survived in the memory of generations to come, in the future, for all time. Nevertheless, the poets in love with life, the heroes and dreamers, never gave up crying out to the Gods and cursing them with rage for excluding us from the elixir of immortality, apparently reserved exclusively for the divine.

If our destiny seems to be no more than to live, wither away and die, why did the Gods give us the ability to love unconditionally beyond our reach across time and dream of a life everlasting? It is said they heard Achilles challenge and taunt the heavens with a similar plight. The chroniclers of his life bear witness to both the divine and mortal blood that ran through his veins, yet he did not share the same destiny, the Holy Grail from the hand of Hebe, as the beautiful soul of the young lover of Eros, Psyche.

Today, science has already discovered the immortal gene, the switch that remains turned off in our DNA that prevents the telomeres from diminishing and wearing out at a cellular level. If this gene could be turned on it would allow us to live on in the same physical body without aging or losing our vitality and basic functions. It is interesting that it would be science, as well, the one who discovered the most powerful agent responsible for turning on this immortal gene. This potential and this gene are inherent in us, are part of our physical construction, not a fairy tale or myth of a long-gone age. What activates it, according to scientific findings, is not so much a substance or secret elixir we must ingest but something surprising and unexpected within us, unrecognized — our common thoughts, our consciousness.

The most advanced studies of our times on genetics and neuroscience continue to offer us convincing and growing evidence that our daily thoughts — even those we do not pay much attention to and run unconsciously without reins behind the curtains of our life's dramas — are what determine and mold our experiences in life. Our thoughts have a real impact on the multitude of physiological processes in our body and determine how we adapt to our environment as well as the experiences we get to choose, engage, and live that define our identity and the quality of our life.

How could it be possible that the key to immortality and eternal life was always hidden inside us? How can it be something so subjective, so within our reach and apparently simple, that at the same time slips away from our grasp? The greatest legendary masters who have survived and are still remembered in history offer us their life's example as a testament of truth that immortality and a life worthy of being remembered throughout time is not mere fantasy but something reachable and real for those who understand what those legendary beings knew and learned and still know. It is true, nevertheless, that such a conquest is the crown of glory of a splendid radical few!

We are reminded, specifically, of Apollonius of Tyana. Apollonius' chronicler Philostratus, the personal historian of Roman Empress Julia Domna, recorded the sage's celebrated last words at his trial before Emperor Domitian and the Roman Senate. The Emperor asks Apollonius whether he realizes that his life and freedom depend completely on the Emperor's decisions. To this Apollonius replies with the epic words of Homer, from *The Iliad*, where Hector of Troy bellows in anguish to Achilles in the battlefield: "Don't you know that you cannot slay me, since I tell you, I am not mortal?"

"And with these words Apollonius vanished from the court, which was the best thing he could do under the circumstances, for the Emperor clearly intended not to question him sincerely about the case."[2]

The question that has escaped us and remained largely unclear to this day is this: What is the art, the Holy Grail for conquering time and reaching immortality? The masters and teachers throughout history have always insisted that the path and the answer are usually very simple. They require, nevertheless, an unwavering dedication to the knowledge and its application in life by our own hand in order to reach our goal.

This art is the craft of the Great Work, where the rough metals of our mortal humanity are transmuted through initiations in the knowl-

---

2   Philostratus, *The Life of Apollonius of Tyana, Vol. 2, Trans. by F.C. Conybeare.* Loeb Classical Library, Harvard University Press. Cambridge, Massachusetts, 1912.

edge. Our base metals are transformed into the purest metal of all that never tarnishes or ages like solid gold.

This ancient and legendary knowledge is the wisdom that recognizes the divine inside each human being simply because we are the creators of our destiny by virtue of our thoughts and their impact on reality. This is the message and teaching of the Master Teacher Ramtha the Enlightened One, the Lord of the Wind, and his School of Enlightenment.

This book you hold in your hands gathers Ramtha's teachings that illustrate the journey one must take to understand the nature of time and how to create our timelines and destiny consciously and intentionally. That is the subject covered in the first part, "Remembering the Future."

Significantly, and what often passes by before us unnoticed, is what we must do to conquer our humanity, riddled with limitations and doomed to the grave. What does it take to become legendary beings, worthy of being remembered beyond time? This is covered in the second part of this book, "To Become the Master of Time, You Must Conquer the Beast."

Ramtha explains that focus is the master key to accomplish the task and offers us various practical ways in which to put it into practice. The third and final part of the book delves into the concept of the river of time and a mind that is frequency specific with the future, how we can reprogram our brain with an immortal dream of metamorphosis, and how the wave of reality can be created and molded from the point of view of a master.

You hold in your hands the first book of Ramtha's knowledge and wisdom of the collection "North Star Ram," published by Hun Nal Ye Publishing. Hun Nal Ye is the name of the Mayan Young God of Corn of our ancestors. Following this title will come more volumes of this special collection covering the subjects of the brain and how to create a lofty life, the art of the Observer and experience as the wellspring of wisdom, and another volume dedicated to awakening into a wonderful life we get to create intentionally and mindfully.

It is important to insist that you read the words of the Master Teacher closely and with great attention and an open mind, finding ways in which to put them to the test in your own life so they become a living experience for you and not just merely words without life. Because as Ramtha states in this book:

"These are very simple little notes but within them hold the secrets to a seventh-level master, a multidimensional entity, an impressive master who has the magic to make things happen."

— *Ramtha*

I leave you in good hands. This is more than a mere book. Its intended objective is to produce in you a sincere, personal contemplation, an experience, and to open widely the doors for your Spirit to fly away with the wings of a butterfly, as Psyche and Eros, in the divine garden of fantastic realism. With your permission, may it be so!

Jaime Leal Anaya
Rainier, Washington, September 3, 2012

PART 1
REMEMBERING THE FUTURE

Song of Praise of What Is Yet to Become

O my beloved God,
Mysterious One,
that of no name,
O, how I celebrate you.
Indeed I celebrate my life,
for I have lived a fine year,
indeed to the greatest of my ability,
indeed of my surrender.
O beloved one,
I have labored towards emancipation
in the bondage
of my flesh.
So be it.
My beloved God,
I give thanks
to my life.
My beloved God,
I give thanks
for the year that unfolds.
May I live it
in surrender.
May I live it
in unlimitedness.

May I live it
beyond the reach
of my mortal death.
So be it.
My beloved God,
O Mysterious One,
I evoke you
to set my soul
on fire.
I evoke you
to release me
from this my flesh,
that that which you are,
Indeed I shall be.
So be it.
To life,
forever and ever
and ever.

1. Creating the Future As the Now

"The way you become immortal
is when you create immortality."
— Ramtha

To live an eternity you must consider the concept of years. You know they are an illusion but to a creating mind they are very real indeed. Time marches on, as if years were a march of a great army that continues marching on. Yet there is no such thing. It is all an illusion. But to an entity that lives in linear space, meaning counting from here to there and that becomes their reality, then time and space are indeed real, and they provide the meaningful highway in which to exist in life. Without time and space, you would not have this life as you have come to know it.

Given that is an acceptance by you that you consider a year a beginning and an end — an alpha and omega, and that time in a year exists — then it would be to your great advantage to begin the ending of the year in a celebration and see it all the way through in a moment. As we have celebrated God, the Mysterious One, with our toast, we have also celebrated your life which is to come. If that is done passionately, then you have created this next year that no thing will bruise or hurt you, that your destiny will be to live that year out.

We cannot say that you are the lords of your reality and negate destiny. You are creators of destiny even when you created it unconsciously. You contemplated death, your ending, worried about your future, and instead you have created a dubious life, a year that is uncertain rather than a year that is grounded in the fortitude of life forces.

Why are you impassioned when we salute God? Because this is alpha and omega. It is a point, an ending of one and a beginning of another. If we wish to celebrate this again, then we start the celebration right now of a year that has yet to unfold and celebrate it as if it has already ended.

Consciousness and energy then is creating reality and we are working within the parameters of your acceptance. Because you accept time, then let us create this year that it unfolds in the name of your God and not in the name of your worry and concern and your fear of death.

26

If we create it in the name of God and create it that it already reached its end, then your destiny will be to live life through the vessel of your God and you will not die nor will you be bruised.

What does an immortal being do? A fledgling immortal is one who is not completely certain, one who has a watch but lives in the Now. I call them fledgling immortals. For you to become such is very simple. All you have to do is create that future as a Now. Create it, celebrate it, and call it forward. When you call it forward in such profound passion, it will be so. Now we have an entity who is beginning to understand that the reason you are here is because you made it through this year. You made it, haphazardly, because you all believed in consciousness and energy but not all the way, not completely. There were points and times and cards that you made and fields you went through,[1] cursing and gnashing your teeth, that brought you here. You just barely made it. This year you make it as a conscious being when you learn that is how it unfolds.

---

1   For a description of Ramtha's disciplines taught at RSE mentioned in this book, such as Fieldwork®, the "power breath" of C&E®, the Neighborhood Walk®, etc., see the Selected Glossary at the end of this book.

If you are an expert recordkeeper of your own proclamation and you review in the year to come its conclusion, then you begin to understand that the way you become immortal is when you create immortality. You will see that by that most impassionate prayer and celebration you experienced those words, indeed, and that is what called it forth.

You don't create immortality based upon your description of immortality. What would your description be? How would you describe immortality? What do you think it is? It isn't any of those things. How could it be? Immortality is beyond description. The frontal lobe in the brain does not have the facility to contemplate it. It does not have the training to contemplate it. The brain is trained to be a timeful being. Mindfulness is also timefulness. Why am I lecturing you on this? Because of your prayer and salutation. Why was it impassionate? Why must you have passion and what is passion? Passion is when you are overcome with the Spirit, the idea, the desire, the voluntariness of what you are saying. And when you surrender to those words and you become them, then you set it in motion because now we have energy, and this concept takes energy to unfold in its most unlimited degree.

The Charitable Act
of Presence and Surrender

"When you sit down to focus because you want to focus, this is your charitable act. When you sit and engage in it — not sitting there thinking about what you should be doing but in complete surrender — it is so sweet and so without limitation that whatever your mind lightly dances upon, becomes."

— *Ramtha*

I want to clarify for you a dimensional mind. This great teaching came about because it was at the end of the year, filled with a great amount of fire and change, struggle and allegiance, commitment and all the necessary things that it takes to cultivate an almost-initiate. All of those emotions that you went through this year are necessary because they fired change in the entity. And change in the entity, no matter how the emotion comes, must happen. The emotion comes pointed in a certain direction for you to make choices. The emotions are there because you are in school and will have to make choices, and those choices are emotional. The emotional aspect wanes but the passionate energy behind it is used to advance you.

At the end of the year everyone is exhausted, afraid I am going to put them in the field again, and then bring them in the hall and make them engage the dance. They think they have it all figured out. Never try to figure me out. At the end of the year, what happened in this great event was that I had students come who volunteered to come. This is not a word that I ever used in my language but I appreciate its root meaning. Volunteer means "want," surrender to the want.

At the end of the year I had students who voluntarily came to an event that others prophesied would be nothing but Fieldwork®. You can tell they were not yet great in their prophecies. They need to come back. They have not passed the prophecy test yet. Those who came did it voluntarily.

Now I have something in a pot, the energy and the surrender, the desire and the commitment of a lot of painful choices they brought with them. And so I have a group of people at the end of the year who come and bring with them all that they have learned all through the year, the rawness and emotional aspects of their nature, those failed romances — won and lost, easy today, easy tomorrow — and all those decisions of trial and error.

I had a group of people in which the most sublime teaching was ready to be given because they volunteered to be here. That meant I didn't have to convince them that they were wonderful or convince them of the measure they should give to consciousness and energy. I did not have to utilize words in repetitive form in order to get them to wake up, other than a "broadsword up against the side of the head."

I had students who, because they volunteered to be here and didn't have to be here, wanted to learn. And I gave them the best of the year's teachings. If I had put them in the field all night long, they would have stayed in the field all night. If I had them dance all day and make masks, they would have danced all day and made masks. This is the prime material that a great God is carved from, this attitude, a voluntary attitude.

How many of you associate the word volunteer with charitable works? You are correct. Why do those two go together? Because good works, as your language would have them, are based upon people with good hearts, and they volunteer their life, their service to be a part of it. That is what makes it charitable. There is no charitableness without the volunteer because the charitable work did not exist prior to the volunteer. The volunteer made the charitable work. This means that the energy of their body, their thoughtfulness, their focus, what they did one day, two days, three days, they gave that energy to a project and gave it without resentment. Volunteers don't have resentment; otherwise they don't volunteer.

We could have a long dissertation on the quality of charitable works. It is a meaning and a definition I want you to understand, for I do not want your consciousness envious and poisoned. We are here to define consciousness until our consciousness becomes kingly in manner and form. And in order for that king and queen to emerge, we must rest ourselves upon the loftiest of thoughts.

I want you to understand this. There are

those of you who can manifest. You create your card in Fieldwork® and you manifest it. You contemplate upon anything and, like magic, it chimes its way into your life. Then there are those of you who struggle and become resentful of the struggle and give up the Great Work. You then have a disbelief in the Great Work and look for someone to tell it to you differently. Here is the reason: Those who manifest the most overtly have the sweetest surrender of all. They are charitable entities, meaning they volunteer. When they sit and focus and learn, they do so not because they have to but because they want to. It is their calling. Then the charitable work is created from their God for them to experience, and that is why it comes easily to them. If you are struggling in your focus, if you are struggling in your manifestation, it is because you are not volunteering. You are not surrendering yourself to do it.

The human being has a story that is tragic. The human being's access to its own immortality has been blocked. The human being's access to its far memory and to its longevity has been blocked. The human being lives in a cage like an animal, and that cage is defined by its intelligence. The knowledge it has declares its parameters of existence. It is like a blind and deaf person, as if a dead entity is moving through life unaware of the life that dances above its head. Human beings are tragic creatures, and yet the tragedy ends when simple secrets are found for their relief.

There would never have been great teachers and indeed great Gods walk among you if it was not a truth that there is a path and a way for your deliverance. Know you that this is the plane of demonstration? Do you know why you are here? You are here to define yourself outside of matter, and when you keep coming back to matter, you have not defined yourself outside of it but rather have surrendered to it.

The key of this teaching in this school is that your consciousness creates your reality, your imprisonment, your lacks, your fulfillments. Everything you have that sits in front of your table is what you have created. The human being's most tragic part is that it will accept its limitations, its blindness, its chemical body. The human will accept the limitations of its flesh rather than volunteer itself for a higher principle, a loftier principle. And the tragedy is that this garment, given an opportunity on the plane of demonstration to awaken, goes through life asleep again.

I want you to understand that I don't keep anything from you that you are not ready to learn so that I can torment you. You just can't learn until you have surrendered to learn. When you surrender to learn is when you say, "I volunteer my life for the loftiest principle of all. I give of myself that I may know that which I cannot know this moment."

When you do, you open the doors and the knowledge rushes toward you. When you sit down to focus because you want to focus, this is your charitable act. When you sit and engage in it — not sitting there thinking about what you should be doing but in complete surrender — it is so sweet and so without limitation that whatever your mind lightly dances upon, becomes. The volunteer is shown mercy, tolerance, love, and extended life. Volunteers have radiant health and the principles of knowing. They have a joy that sings from their being because they have volunteered their life.

If an entity sits for fifty-three years in the lotus position contemplating its misspent youth, he will have relived his life for another fifty-three years. That is boring and mundane. However, if the volunteer in the principle of the Great Work sits and focuses for fifty-three years, their focus would be upon pushing the boundaries that enclose them. Their focus is to break through, and one fine morn they will break through. The brain will start working on a higher level, those lofty thoughts will start manifesting, and all of the charitable work will finally pay off for the one who did it, only because they volunteered their life for it.

2. Looking Forward in Retrospect Creates the Future Time

"What can be done backwards in consciousness can be done forward in consciousness. You are the Gods, the creators of reality."
— *Ramtha*

You can't possibly understand what is at the end of these teachings. So far the teachings have served you greatly. There is not one entity that has not benefited from these teachings, even those who have left the school bitterly. They are so bitter they still cannot change, yet continue to talk about the school. This school has served everyone by all the things that you have heard here and all the steps that you have taken in your field. Let us observe for a moment: Are you the same person that first came to this audience?

If you have evolved, and clearly you can recognize it and can see in looking backward what you could not see then, do you not find that an irony? Looking backwards where? The name of your year that has passed is a number. It is not the Year of the Monkey. Time exists in your head. When you look back at your life in this last year, where did you go for the source of your information? In your memory. What you know now, you did not know then. If you look back on "then" — which is now, but was then — you didn't know what you know now.

A year forward exists now. What does the year forward possess that you don't know now? Do you not consider this a worthy question? What does the year forward hold that you do not know now? What kind of year is it? What is it that you want this year?

We are headed into the Year of the Snake. What do you know now that you didn't know but attempted to know? The year that comes already is. It already is. It has already happened. It is not the Year of the Monkey. It is the Year of the Snake. It has already happened. What is it that you did that year that went by so fast you didn't know it happened?

This is a mind twister. The Ram gives you a twister in the mind, and some of you give up and scratch your rear ends and play with your hair because you can't keep up with the thought. But the thought, by God, is what creates it all. And if you cannot reason, if you cannot reach for that thought and cannot contemplate that it already is, then how do you expect it to ever be?

What is to say that the Year of the Snake has not already happened? Where I come from, it already has. The potential that lies ahead of you is vast. If you were to go outside and look into the midnight blue and you saw that the sky in its darkness was dusted with shiny things, sparkling gems, some dancing quietly in the sky, you would see that your life in the year ahead is like that sky. Each one of those lights represents a chosen path. They represent an experience. You can go this way, that way, or this way. And if you look at it, you can understand that if you make certain choices by looking in this direction, then you are going to see that direction and you are going to miss this other direction. If you look over here and you keep focused on that light over there, you are going to miss these others.

Your life is like the sky at night, filled with mystery and silence and opportunity. Every light possesses itself an unknown adventure and quietly beckons your gaze in its direction. When I looked at the sky at night, I thought I was looking in God's treasure-trove. So vast and so beautiful was the sky in those days, it taught me that if I focused on this direction, I was narrowed and missed all of the other directions. I realized that this was an unspoken teaching about my life and therefore I engulfed the whole of the sky, beyond the North Star. I took its entire gaze into my life and dared for it all to be lived, and I did.

So, my sleepy little human beings, when I pose this riddle your way, I am getting you to bounce out of logic into the mystical. I am challenging you to forward your mind into the unheard-of. I am challenging you to keep up with my thought, and by doing so you have to have the same thought. If you have the same thought and your attention is focused in that direction, then it is that thought whose destiny must come to pass in your life.

I want you to wake up and contemplate. The year that has ended was filled to the brim of things to do. And did you do them? I expect you did, for in looking back you accomplished and learned and were filled, and now you know. If this was backward in time and I asked you this question, "Dare you look forward to the end of next year," you would say, "I am looking forward to the end of next year and I get impressions. It is as if I have lived them, as if I have known them."

If you said that, you would say, "But, Master, it is only because I lived that year. If I go back in my mind and contemplate the beginning of the year, I have already lived that year. So if I have to go back to the beginning and remember what it was like, oh, yes, I can remember at that moment wanting these things to happen but was unsure of myself. But on reflection I see that they all came to pass and indeed I changed."

So is this really a fair question? No, it isn't.

And yet what can be done backwards in consciousness can be done forward in consciousness. Don't you know you are the Gods, the creators of reality? Your tragedy is that you accept your malady and do not challenge the parameters of the mystical.

Now it is the end of next year. You have already lived the end of next year. What did you experience and how did you change? Can you do that? Take out a piece of paper, and this paper you want to keep. It is a log of your journey. I want you to remember all that happened to you next year. I want you to remember what made you change and what it was you changed into; and, remember, this is the end of next year. You may put your blinders on and focus. I will give you music, and I want everyone to participate. I will show you how magic works in consciousness without time.

When you start focusing on the end of next year — which your logical mind says hasn't even really begun — if you focus on its end you will know the journey of where you have trod and what you have accomplished. You will know it. And all I want you to do is write it down, no matter what comes to you in its vision. Write it down, because we are going to take a look at the night sky and we are going to see it in a different perspective.

The Dream of Nature — The Highest Form of Natural Magic

"The human being who transcends
its personal tragedy will do so by
transcending the tragedy of its
blindness, its limitation and self-imposed
imprisonment, and awakening into the
dream of nature."
                    — Ramtha

Let us reason what you have done in your acceptance and not your folly. Remember the teaching of the tree. What does the tree do in winter? It dreams the dream of spring. What does the caterpillar do when it makes its silken bed and goes to its pallet? Dreams the dream of the butterfly. The tree in winter, in its deep slumber — while its boughs are filled with the great white silence and the bitter wind of a blue northern blows through its delicate fingers — is asleep, I tell you, slumbering in a dream of long thought. It dreams the dream of spring and of a new and beautiful garment and delicate fingers that grow to grasp the morning light. And in nature what it has dreamt in its slumber, behold, it becomes in its spring and upon its wakening.

All of nature resounds with this truth if you have but the eyes open to see it. If you pass a tree and nod to it and contemplate its dream, look at it. It is asleep and it dreams of a life that it knows will surely come again. All of nature in its splendid evolution has this remarkable ability. It is the power of transmutation and regeneration.

Who does not believe in the tree of winter and the tree of spring? And who does not believe in the caterpillar and indeed the butterfly? Who does not believe in the great fish that fights its way to give birth to itself again in the spring? Don't you know that what we have done here in school is the highest form of natural magic? Don't you know that you are students who have dreamed the dream of your new year to come? By doing this you have been unified with nature, not going against the principle of the natural law but indeed immersed yourselves in it. Nature's very principle you have become.

Let us reason this. The human being who transcends its personal tragedy will do so by transcending the tragedy of its blindness, its limitation and self-imposed imprisonment, and awakening into the dream of nature. What we have done here in school is not imagined simply a folly. You have been taught the virtue of a common word — uncommon in my time — to volunteer. To volunteer is to become charitable, and to become charitable means that you have dedicated this moment as a student, volunteered your mind, its imagination, and your time and its space to participate in a natural science. The world at large, the woods in midnight, and the spring in all of its flora and fauna, its birds and beautiful butterflies have all been the fruit of such a moment as this. You did not simply imagine the year to come but you practiced the natural art of dreaming it into being. That is what we did. You have been part of a natural law.

Those of you who surrendered and participated and fully became all that was remembered of what is yet to come are now participating in a powerful consciousness called immortality, the unfoldment of the dreams of winter into spring. Outside of this training, in your stupid arrogance you never knew that the Unknown God in its profound wisdom was abundant even in your backyard. You who were so enslaved and imprisoned in fulfilling the needs of your flesh never stopped to contemplate the magic of a tree and how it unfurls its new garment in the spring. You never paused to contemplate what is the progenitor, its stimulus of growth and continuity.

Who do you think is going to teach you, and what do you think they would teach you in order to wake you up? They would never teach you anything outside the natural principles of nature itself because that be life. They would never teach you silly things, never teach you only words for you to mimic and remember. How do you think you would learn of how the masters cast their spell upon the future? How is the spell cast? What form of magic must you do in order to create a fantastic future? How can an entity look through the year to come as if it were looking back on it and remembering minute details so accurately? Because they dreamed the dream and their consciousness is in alignment with the principal cause. You are alive but you have been dead. You are dead to nature's everlasting magic.

Henceforth you will review time in perhaps a different fashion. How did you create your years before? You didn't. In a drunken slumber the idolaters of the image — you — danced and drank and told lies, and then you screamed and blew party horns and that was it. That was to foretell your year, whatever it would be. And look at how you set it up. If one celebrates time, one must celebrate time as a magician, not a fool. If you are to celebrate time, you must do so knowing full well that however you celebrate it, whatever means you celebrate it with, become the chains that hold you to that concept for as long as the celebration was meant to last.

Let us reason why I asked you to follow me in your mind. Let us jump ahead and remember what has not yet been. Let us dare to become outrageous. Look at the sky. Can you see all of the stars at once? Does the past resemble the future? Do the past and the future exist as a unit called Now? Do you simply focus linearly upon a parcel of that and, as you focus upon it, is the only part that unfolds in linear time? Time and space are filled with predetermination but from an ignorant point of view.

To have taken you on a journey forward and remembered it backwards is an art of consciousness. It is not the art of the reasonable mind. It is an art of consciousness, the fire of God, your God, whose tongue speaks through you in thoughtful forms. It comes through you and says, "Let me show you. Let us see. Let me, for I am always."

When the tree dreams the dream in winter, it is dreaming the dream not of winter but of spring. When the caterpillar dreams the dream, the caterpillar doesn't dream of a caterpillar; it dreams the dream of the butterfly.

Before, you have associated time with present beingness. And what is present beingness? If you feel bad, you are giving time only more of what you presently are. Rather, take time and push it to its most outrageous borders to where your mind can no longer make the visions that are necessary for one to have inward vision and fire of focus. If you press your consciousness to such extraordinary lengths, then time fulfills that vision rather than the same vision of sameness, which is tiredness, limitation, fatigue, sickness, and illness. That sameness of being is age and lethargy, the sameness of being which is sensual, physical, and the structure of the mundane. When you think of time, you think of time only in the present context and the greatest form of limitation rather than the art of dreaming it.

Let us reason. If a worm can grow oriental fans and fly away, a human being can dream the dream of Spirit in its most illuminating body and float away.

3. Rising Out of Time and Becoming an Immortal

"If your consciousness is powerful enough to have dreamed the dream of what is yet to come as if it already is and remembered it in clear detail, then you are rising out of time and becoming an immortal."

— Ramtha

This teaching was powerful because I instructed you to follow me into the impossible, into the illogical. I asked you to become outrageous, to volunteer your mind and get it away from the predictable into the unpredictable. In doing so, we have created a dream. We have dreamed the dream this winter's night of spring and summer, midsummer's eve, and the magic of moments of fall and its golden splendor, the sweet kiss of cold when it comes, and a moon that waxes and wanes. Oh, don't you know that what I have taught you is the secret of life and its immortal evolution?

This is not imagination; it is forecasting self. It is a divination of self, indeed the elaboration of self. It is taking a common mind and making it uncommon. Don't you know we have dreamed the dream of the year to come, for I say it has already been. When the leaves begin to bud, the buds swell in the branches and their gentle fingers, and they are pregnant with their new body. Those beautiful leaves of such bright, luscious green begin to burst open from their small little shell. Don't you know that the tree has already been this? Don't you know that this is simply the rendering of what, deep in its sleep, it has done?

The magic is not in the leaves but in that which created them, the pulsation of the life force itself. To dream the dream, to forecast it in the outrageous, is to set it in the womb of

God, and it is. I speak this with passion because it is so close to you. The words that I utter are closer to you than the hair on your head. This science is vital and is the wine that wakes you up. If you know how to use this and you dream this dream and speak it forth, discuss it, and it takes literary form, then you know the magic of a master who no longer treats time as if it were something to be laid, as an egg that is laid day after day after day and has no expression of change to it.

Your destiny happened tonight. Your destiny happens every moment that you stop the sensual acts in your body and allow your mind to rest upon a principle. Wherever your mind focuses in the sky, whatever part of itself it focuses upon, then that will be your journey.

I tell you, you are more than flesh and blood. There is an entity inside you that transcends all of this, and to dream its mindful dream is to dream genius. To dream about this entity and its unfathomable consciousness is to dream genius, and that affords change. Don't be afraid to change. Don't be afraid to lose your scales. Don't be afraid. Surrender, dream it into being, and it will come just as spring will come.

This is natural magic in its purest form, so innocent. Do not think folly what you have done, make laughter at what you have done. Leave in humble reverence to the power of what you have done and give thanks that you know how to do it. And when you look at a tree, know that the tree is doing the same thing. The next time you see a caterpillar, look at it. Soon it will be changed and your envious heart will weep when it flies away.

Consciousness and energy creates the nature of all reality. Within the womb of that most broad and sweeping statement comes that time and space exist. Time and space do not encapsulate consciousness and energy but the reverse. If your consciousness is powerful enough to have dreamed the dream of what is yet to come as if it already is and remembered it in clear detail, then you are rising out of time and becoming an immortal. Remember, if you understand this science in your deepest focus, you should rush to it as a volunteer. Rush to this focus to volunteer your moment to dream the focused dream to the most outrageous principle. To have focused on the common, to have focused upon the mundane, squanders time because it only repeats itself, and you only get repeated what you have thought.

When you have a lofty thought, one that you pluck out from beyond the North Star, a thought that challenges mental construction, now we are coming alive. There never has to be an end to your life as long as you are natural magic, as long as you and nature are one and the same and you abide by its principle. The principle of life and death is a harsh principle indeed, and it is the realism of nature, the survival of the fittest, as you will see. And yet with that harsh law comes redemption and freedom because in understanding, what amongst you is everlasting? The tree and the rock, the sky and the quicksilver water. The water evaporates, and though you weep and say "I am without the elixir," yet I tell you it has changed form and it is the cloud above your head. If you are a fortunate person and dreamed the dream of that cloud raining pure water in your mouth, I say to you, thunder will roar and it will rain again and the water will be born again. It is the natural law.

What is everlasting in nature? The meat-eaters perish. Those that come as a high intelligent form are a flash in time. They come and go quickly, but the rock of ages, the tree of life, the sky and its everlasting nature, the waters of life that provide the vine with the wine that refreshes and subdues are those which are eternal.

If you know how to do this and revere what you have done, you have found the secret to everlasting life because the butterfly only has to continue to dream. The tree can dream about the spring two thousand years from today. And when it dreams of the spring in two thousand years, it will live again and that spring will surely come. If you are the rulers of your destiny, then your destiny is only as great as your knowledge and your ability to exercise it. Your ability to exercise it can only give you wisdom. Your ability and your desire to exercise it qualify that wisdom.

Entities say that there is a secret to imagination. Imagine, if you will, that what you want to do is already done and, like magic, you will find that it will be done straightaway and with the greatest of ease it will be accomplished. But that is only equal to your ability to imagine. There is a profound truth in that. Imagination is like a caged bird living in a gilded cage. Imagination is like the beautiful dove, white with blood-red eyes. Imagination calls for freedom, calls for expression. Its wings were built to fly, and yet the gilded cage of logic keeps it locked away. So one imagines, but its logic says, "I forbid you to come, forbid you to fly. It is only my imagination." Tonight, this is not imagination. This is powerful dreaming and this dream manifests. So be it.

The highlight of your year you have dreamed. The subtle natures of that dream you have not put down, for you have not recognized them. The subtle nature of the dream you have not remembered. You have only remembered the highlights of the year, what you wanted to remember. You do not remember how you remembered, nor the experience and the runners that came from nowhere to bring about that memory. You have only remembered the highlights. The mother remembers the child who was just born on her breast but does not remember how it got there.

These things come and they come in mysterious winds, through mysterious forces, some predictable, most unpredictable. But what they deliver is what you will always remember. Your year will be filled with a mixture of comings and goings, of strangers and mysterious things, of new knowledge unexplained, of incidents heartfelt, some very painful, others in bliss. But the comings and goings of entities of your life and the comings and goings of the seasons bring about what you will remember and what you have remembered, except you won't remember that that is how they got here.

The Great Work Sealed under the Pentagram

"If there is one symbol that already exists in the subconscious mind that has the power and authority over the netherworld, it is this symbol. It means knowledge, transmutation. It means the height of human expression, of human form, and it is a shield."

— Ramtha

Now we are going to seal this work. We are going to place a seal on all the things that you have seen of the year to come and written down. The seal is a symbol, and it is a symbol that both accentuates and protects. This symbol is the pentagram. I want you to know that this is not a sign of Lucifer, and any of you who are superstitious enough to think that should not make the sign. This is a powerful, evoking symbol, and we only lay this to certain things in this school. The year that is coming up will be the year of the pentagram, for the work will be done under its symbol. It is quite illuminating and quite expansive.

Take out your first sheet of paper of your dreams. Boldly, across the face of every one of the pages you have recorded your memories of the year to come, make a fine-line pentagram, as if all that you have done is under its shadow. Make a fine-line pentagram across the entire face of every sheet as if it is a shadow and make it very slowly, with reverence. The pentagram is a symbol of the human. If you look at it, you will see a star that has a head, two arms, and two legs.

Individuals in your society that are revered are called stars and their emblems are pentagrams. They are unaware of its meaning but its pursuit and its final acclaim were worth it all. To be called the star is to be called the pentagram. This symbol is the symbol of the human in its most knowledgeable form. It means that the star shines, and if the star shines it means that there is a fire within it that is lit with knowledge. This symbol is so powerful it surpasses the visible-light spectrum.

Because of this symbol's power to the sub-conscious mind, those in religious authority have gone to great lengths since the birth of one God and one religion to extinguish all lifeforms who understood its meaning. Its meaning is so powerful it overrides the authority of the church; it overrides the authority of dogma and superstition. The greatest way to destroy any one thing is to shroud it in mystery and fear and proclaim it to all adherents that those who gaze upon it will be consumed by the devil, that those who wear it are worshipers of the lord of this world.

And of course it gets the reputation, and the ignorant remain ignorant, are born, live, die, and never understand their true origins. If there is one symbol that already exists in the subconscious mind that has the power and authority over the netherworld, it is this symbol. It means knowledge, transmutation. It means the height of human expression, of human form, and it is a shield.

So now we have sealed the year to come with a five-pointed star. We have sealed it with the pentagram, and that means that the subconscious mind acknowledges what it has created and gives right to its form. The pentagram means it surpasses the image.

So what we have put down we have protected from corruption, protected from erosion. We have made what you have written sacred.

Perhaps one day all of you will wake up and realize that the most meager of things that you think, and how you formulate them into words, manifest. Perhaps you will understand that when you are put to the task of regeneration and re-creation, you will find that it deserves an in-depth and serious thought on your part. Now that we have sealed your dream with this shield and this protection, it is as good as over. So be it.

PART 2
TO BECOME THE MASTER OF TIME, YOU MUST CONQUER THE BEAST

Prayer of Deliverance

O my beloved God,
that which you be,
the mystery,
the myth,
the enchantment,
my God, at times I disbelieve,
indeed doubt
that which you be.
I am a pitiful and wretched being
who has designed my world
by degrees and depth and solidity.
O my God,
indeed in my ignorance
how could I have ever
known that which you be,
except in the things that I wanted,
indeed that I needed.
O Mysterious One,
I beckon you
to whatever form be you,
or formless be you,
press nearer to my heart,
indeed my brain,

indeed my world,
that the brittleness of myself
may begin to shatter.
O my beloved God,
for indeed what be I
without that which created me.
So be it.
To life.

4. The Extraordinary As a Talisman of the Future and the Art of Creation

"I tell you, the person who is lord of the day is not the beast but the one who creates the day."
— *Ramtha*

My beloved people, I want to talk to you about your boxes that you live in, the grid.

How many of you have had an extraordinary experience? The extraordinary experience can be a small miracle which was unexpected but desired. It could be something you focused upon, created in one vast nothing in a practice session, perchance, or in one of your early moments when you were in deep thought about something that you needed, wanted, or were just observing. How many of you have had an extraordinary experience? Extraordinary means it is still ordinary. It is within the grid and can be defined by memory but is external to what your grid normally is.

Would you say then that that experience could be called a truth that cannot be defined in normal terms? Would you also say that it was enough stimulus for you to devote yourself further to the study of extraordinary abilities? This is important because everyone has to have a little small something — a crumb — from the table of nothing in order to give them the motivation. They must stand as a cartouche, an emblem, a medallion, a memorial of their experience to that which is the bane of society or a truth that they can say, "I have had this happen to me. No one else can explain it, but because of it, it shall be my talisman in the face of my own self-doubt."

Has that extraordinary experience been a talisman to you? Crumbs fall from one vast nothing into the introduction of the sincere student to be a testament to them that their God is alive and well. It shows them that they can access one vast nothing when self-doubt or the doubt of the grid becomes prevailing. Has this been your testament?

We are going to talk about the miraculous — the miraculous — not in terms of getting things but the lifeline to such a source, to an immutable Source. It is not about things. It is about feeling special from something extraordinary — that you feel blessed, you feel honored — that you have been singled out for something to happen to you from a source that supersedes the senses and all intelligence. You could always lump that under or say you had a calling from God or from a master. It doesn't matter. All of you have experienced the opportunity to feel as if something, or some "nothing," knows that you exist and that you are important, because you made a difference in the extraordinary — "extra-ordinary."

This is interesting. It does not mean that something happened to you, that the thing itself is not supernatural. It is ordinary but the way in which it occurred is "extra" because this is not a program in the grid. There is noplace to where this experience has been allowed in your grid. This isn't the program that runs twenty-four hours in your day. It came outside of the program and yet the thing itself was ordinary. Those are the things of the miraculous self and they start small, always. They start small, never big, because big ones create disbelief and small ones create marvelous acceptance.

What did that crumb break off from — what large dinner plate and what did it hold — that this fragment fell off into your bands and into your life? Wouldn't you like to see the whole platter? Yes, anything begging at a table would.

This is necessary for the sincere beginning student. This happens to people in everyday life but rarely. These events often at one time were acceptable, and people were called gifted if that happened to them. This acceptance has sort of been diminished, programmed out, and ridiculed. Very few incidents happen to the ordinary rabble out in the marketplace because the rabble doesn't want anything extraordinary. They just want to survive and be accepted. That is not extraordinary. Extraordinary means that you would be ousted from the approval of your peers if it happened to you.

No one wants anything to happen that would cause them embarrassment and humiliation and put them in a rough spot, to be certain. No one wants to explain their mental or emotional abilities or what their mother did or didn't do to them. These come as little runners. They are wee little entities. They are thoughtfully and intentionally given in unconditional love and received in marvelous astonishment, but with acceptance.

These are the gifts of a great and wise God and also a great and wise teacher. The reason they come this way is to begin to sit in the corner of that which is supreme within you and as immutable evidence in the face of a grid, a peer group, or civilized world. If you ever had to or someone made you have to choose, you would never want to trade that extraordinary experience for the whole world, because that is a lifeline to something enormous, vast, and eternal. Those manifestations are intentional. They help you in this school to slowly build confidence in yourself to do certain disciplines that are, for the most part, formless and without structure and cannot be defined by the intelligent mind. They are only parts of what could be called memory and, for the most part, memory cannot remember "nothing."

This is an arduous task, because you can listen to all the words in the world and I am certain that you would find much more excellent orators than I, but their words are empty. They are like the hulls of a loaf of bread but there is nothing inside. For a world that hungers not for the word but for the bread of life, then the only way that a person can eat of the bread of life is to have the crumbs of the bread of life so they begin to taste it. As they begin to taste it, that is the only thing — save for a splendid rare few — that fires the internal engine of passion and devotion to a work that cannot be weighed or measured, that cannot be shown at the marketplace but is etheric and eternal. These crumbs have to fire the engines of your passion and devotion because without your wanting to engage in the discipline, engage in a work that you can't see the rewards, you can't take and put them into your treasury department. You cannot pay your mortgages with it yet.

We are looking at devoting yourself to something in a world that cries out for dollars and cents and that that should be the only motivation of the human being. This is a difficult wall to come against in teaching you. This wall only comes down little by little in preserving the entity that lives on the other side of the wall by sending to them enough knowledge and trust. Then they slowly begin to allow a brick, a stone, at a time to crumble down and partake of the crumbs from the table and want more. If the entity on the other side of the wall says, "I want more," I tell them, "You will get it but you must remove all these stones." If the miraculous acceptance stands as a talisman — as immutable truth that where these crumbs came from, greater and larger things exist — then with a passion, by their own efforts, they will remove the wall and the barrier that keeps them from the eternal Source.

What indeed am I telling you? I am telling you that reality, as clay, exists all around you, is inside of you. It is that which holds this clay in a womb. And the tool that molds the clay is a focused thought, a focused thought that must supersede the ordinary. And that is how we begin, with focus upon extraordinary things. Extraordinary things are known. They are in memory but are ordinary. They are just "extra" to you.

When I observe you, I observe entities that

very much have strong affection for the teachings and for me because the teachings and I are one and the same. They have strong affections for the school, and yet having had these crumbs, these extraordinary little miracles that you cannot really explain away, I still find a disease of lethargy in you. The disease of lethargy is this: You would rather wake up, arise every morning like you always have from the very first day you were born, go through your day struggling, hating, resenting, despising, being envious, trying to be clever, manipulative, stealing, dishonoring yourself, hypocritical, bearing false witness, and then saying the teachings don't work because you didn't get any manifestations. You would rather elect to live that kind of life, being a slave to not only your grid but the habits that define you. You would rather live every single day of your life in that body, in that state of mind, and in that contracted field than to change that life and begin with the devotion, "My day begins as I create it. Before, the day was there and I had to support it to support myself."

That is why most people don't like getting up early because the day only means another day of monotonous drudgery, which some of you still hold onto. You haven't given it up because somewhere it has not yet occurred to you that the very teachings that you honor, and the disciplines that have been arduous in coming — and this is the shocking case to some of you, not I — that there are those of you who don't even want to apply them unless you are here at school, and this is like going to church.

You dress up to go to church to hear the preacher deliver the sermon in which you nod and yell, "Hallelujah. Indeed, so be it." And you get up and instead of singing, you dance and enjoy yourself, you commune, frolic around, and engage in social events. The rawness of this school, which is so basic without any frivolity to it at all, has become a social event where you must come in order to get stimulated so that you can create while you are in my presence. But the moment you go home tomorrow is another day that you don't want to apply what you have been taught, which is the very key to the kingdom of heaven. There are those of you who don't want to do this because you don't want to change.

Let us go back to this marvelous little miracle accepted. As I told you, that was a crumb from something larger and it was sent intentionally to you as a talisman, that you could remember this fondly. When other people are sharing their experiences, you remember this little miracle. When you begin to self-doubt, this talisman will always stand up as a very small, little thing in opposition to the giant grid, the looming monster in all of you. This little angel, this entity, will stand there illuminated in front of the beast in order to say, "But what about me?"

If you were creators of your day, this is how you would go about it. If you were very, very sincere, you would first understand that the greatest moments of creation come early in the morning before all of the clutter starts hitting the airwaves. Early in the morning means that no one is calling you on the telephone, no one is yakking or spewing garbage at you. It is quiet, nothing needs you. You are unneeded, something that some of you cannot possibly swallow. Aloneness means that you are not needed, but that is what it takes to go through this school. You arise not because I told you to but that you know it is the finest, most refreshing moment, since this is the day that you are going to be awake all day. You are going to be moving through the clouds and veils of your grid and all the people that are in your life. You are not going to get anything or do anything unless you contact several of them to get their approval because they constitute your grid. And you will never want to do anything that goes against the grid because you are not you; they are you.

You move through all of this and you hope at the end of the day that this day was productive, or perhaps it was counterproductive. You survived another day and you just want it to be over with so the evening will come and you can be entertained because you think you deserve it. You don't deserve it. You just deserve to have more habits and gossip, more sharing and more life, which is nothing but the beast. Then you like to stay up late at night because you don't have to work; in the day, you have to.

The wise entity — and there are only a handful in this school — doesn't "have to" get up. You get up because something inside you says, "It is time." And passion and a natural desire will wake you up. You get up and say, "To this day I am lord of my life," and this is the day that you do it.

When you go to slumber at night, you remove your clothing, your garments, or you wear seductive garments or the appropriate nightcap and gown. When you go to the Void, you don't wear anything — not physically, mindfully. And in order to create a day that supersedes your grid and all of those people in your life that you have to account for, you have to strip it all away. You can apply the power breath to clear, go deep into the Void with the correct posture, and learn to focus and fall deeper and deeper into it, or blow deeper and deeper into nothing — nothing, I tell you — formless beingness, and the deeper you go, the more naked you will become.

In other words, your image cannot follow you into the deep hollows of the Void. And if you insist on going there, little by little the image is stripped away, the beast is stripped away. As you find a very peaceful place, you stop for a moment and surrender to it, which means you are surrendering the beast, the grid, what you think, what time it is, what hour it is, is the cock crowing outside, what you are going to do today. You don't think; you surrender all that has constituted you to become a formless, nonthinking being. You can say, "I am," and that is the only description. It is not, "I am George. I am not Araxis. I am not — " No, those are the names of what you have been. In this place you must be naked, "I am," so everything leaves, and that is surrender.

Why is this so hard for you? Because you have such a beast, such a program, approval, and arrogance by which you live. You have your face you have to live by, your husbandman, your wife, the criteria of all of this gridwork that is an illusion. And to give it all up, to disillusionize your husbandman, your wife, your lover, your friends, your children, your sister and your brother, your neighbor, your cousin, your grandparents, your great-grandparents, the mayor, the state, the traffic — what have I missed? — all of these are the same. They must be disillusionized. They cannot exist because they are the trappings of the identifiable self, and the identifiable self is limited by virtue of its grid.

This grid has created all of your days and all of your nights. That is the reason why nothing really extraordinary has ever happened. When you really wanted something and finally got it, you have always been bored with it. You never really love anyone too long because you tire of them. That is because you don't love yourself. It had to be orgasmic, very little cosmic; mostly orgasmic and needy survival. You are bored with them but you don't know how to tell them that. You see, that is the self, that empty, completely negative — negative, not in a diminished sense but lacking. This lacking, needy, possessive tyrant is the beast that has the identity of your name. It does not create the extraordinary. If it did, it would undermine its very existence.

The extraordinary comes from a subtler, deeper place. And I tell you, this sounds easy and it is. It is the simplest thing you could ever do. Surrender is taking it to the altar of God, leaving it all behind, and being naked, naked. Can you be naked? Can you disillusionize the people that you fought so hard to hold onto? Can you disillusionize them, forget about them for however long you go into eternity? Do you dare do that or should you console them because you feel guilty that you did it? I tell you, the person who is lord of the day is not the beast but the one who creates the day.

The surrender is so sweet. It is, as I have taught you, a feeling of expansion and floating, a feeling of I am-ness. Isn't it remarkable that in the time that you experience this, you are not concerned with all of the habits, the things you would normally think about, and they don't exist? They don't.

Why do you have to become naked? Because your greatest ideal should be this formless state, naked in identity. When you are, you will have the ability, with no grid but a pure focused thought, to focus on a joyful life, a joyful day. You can surrender, and in the surrender of nothingness you can have the feeling of exuberance, and that exuberance in that day will manifest as joy, a sublimeness of Spirit or genius. Perhaps that day you want an unusual thought, a thought strong enough to take you away from the mundane and uplift your day and help the cracks of change broaden in you.

I am telling you, to go to this place is where the crumbs come from. You get exactly what you deserve and according to the way that you are dressed, dressed not in garments of light, not in garments of gold, but no garments at all, meaning no identity — I am.

Initiation into a Place
Not Governed by Time

*"The truth is, as in the initiations in
the ancient schools, all the testing that
occurred prior to the initiation was to
bring the student into a deeper level of
consciousness, to get them more naked
so that they would be unlimited in their
capacities to manifest the extraordinary."*
— *Ramtha*

Let us examine for a moment how befitting
this would be, because if it were up to our image
we would not get anything extraordinary, just
things moving around on the grid. The extraordinary comes from a different power. It comes
from that very place that I have just taught you
to go, which means that the pathway is open for
you to go there. It also means that any miraculous and beautiful thing brought into your life
will never come through your image. You must
come to a place of complete surrender. The
more guarded you are going there, the more
clouded and cluttered the thought will be.

Here is an example. At the great Assay event, there were entities who made remarkable changes in their life because of a procedure I put them through. I felt, if I may use the word, that the group as a whole, because of a splendid few, was ready for an intense initiation. I put them through it because I wanted them to begin to reach the deeper level of that which I have always taught, have always loved, and indeed have always represented. I wanted them to see that the miraculous place does not come from wishing and wanting but from absolute know-ingness, a state not governed by time.

There were entities that went the whole time of the initiation but got very few rewards because they were so interested in the sacrifices they made. As they sat there, they became the martyrs to their own sacrifice so that became their reality, and the rewards were nominal. The reward was already happening, martyr-dom. There were others who thought it was a holiday and that it was a campout situation. They did not have what it takes to fire it all the way home, to have the opportunity to squeeze out of them greatness, a consciousness born of fire that was burnished like the phoenix and will live forever. There were a few who got to a place that was timeless, indeed, and remarkably they changed. The change filled their countenance and it was bright. There was an ancient awe about them, the serious ones. There were also the social entities who go to-and-fro all the time, who move around, socialize, talk, who really are primitive. But there were a few — oh, my God, the flowers that grew — they changed.

A few of those few did one thing that is a cardinal rule to remember not to do: to share their changes with their friends and find approval. This happened, and I will be most candid with you, the most obvious were their habits. We are going to talk about habits but, in particular, what was obvious within them and, to the external world, their changes. As they talked about their changes, as you always do in your circle of friends, you are asking for permission to change. You are expressing and sharing, but sharing isn't even a proper word. You are throwing it out on the table for every part of you that lives around you to have their say and their opinion. A few of you could not hold the blessed event, and for the sake of keeping yourself together and acceptable, you went back.

There is nothing wrong with that. That doesn't mean that you are bad but it is a sign of how weak you are to a beast that rules your life. The devotion here is not to this hall but to the hall within you, the place where something great and magnificent resides, and it does not matter what the world thinks of you. Inevitably you will become lights, as you already have been, something polished and beautiful for the world to respect when they think so badly of you. Regardless of the world, it should never have mattered because the world is the material place, the place and the kingdom of things, the known realities. You in effect could not live with the change that was unlimited, that indeed freed you and a whole host of energy that you had locked up to create more marvelous things, and greater, more extraordinary things in your life. In fact, you were seduced back and you are the one who created it.

You didn't really change at all. You went back to pleasing the circle of yourself, which is all the people in your life that you have to answer to, check up on, get approval and disapproval from, an okay. You can say that this is honor amongst friends. I would never have a friend who did not absolutely adore me the way that I already was, because prostitution is not meant by whoring; there is also the whoring of the mind. And then there were the other few that the change crested and it began to grow deep roots in the person. There was a wonderful power to them that is innocent somehow. Things happen to them quicker, their thoughts seem to manifest more expediently, they are getting grander thoughts, and they can bring about the extraordinary things just because they have played with the concept. Notice I said played? In other words, they have taken the simplicity of this great teaching and, through their devotion, have put it in their own laboratory with simple things. They have intentionally thought of a person and that person manifested, intentionally thought of other things and it occurred, small things, things that wisely they do because it is marvelously acceptable. You do not accept, nor will your image accept, the supernatural — not yet — but it does tolerate extraordinary happenings.

So what about this initiation? It was really brief but it said a lot about the person to themselves. It did. You can go through an initiation and sustain the initiation, and if you didn't know what you were looking for or how to know, it would seem like everyone passed the test. The truth is, as in the initiations in the ancient schools, all the testing that occurred prior to the initiation was to bring the student into a deeper level of consciousness, to get them more naked so that they would be unlimited in their capacities to manifest the extraordinary. Unless they got there, they could not manifest it on their own.

The initiations were to prepare just to get the entity to be able to manifest on an extraordinary level. The discipline of Fieldwork® is extraordinary. What about then what comes after extraordinary? What are some terms? Supernatural, Absolute Elsewhere, fantastic realism, infinite reality. So to get my students just to manifest the extraordinary has been an arduous task, because the student leaves here its ability to do this and doesn't even get up to change the day, doesn't even get up to motivate itself above its system.

The Caste System You Live In

*"The students in the ancient schools were
often groups within groups, and there were
the sublime that mediocrity didn't even
know existed. In the outer world that is
how the caste system began and still exists
to this day."*
— *Ramtha*

There was something rotten, the smell of carrion, that occurred in the land of Indus after I left. And the priests did this. There was a caste system introduced into the country. In the caste system there were the poor, the illiterate, mediocrity, the have-nots, and then there were secular groups that were divinely and richly given to. This caste system seemed like a very mean system. In fact, it is. However, the wisdom that it was created for originally was this: The caste system developed from later concepts of the ancient schools. Every mother wanted her splendid daughter not to have to build a dowry in order to be married off to some wretched little boy that lived in the next county. Every

83

father had his favorite son. The special daughter and the favorite son often bore signs, and the highest honor that could be paid to a house was to have one of their children accepted into an ancient school.

The ancient school qualified its students, obviously, and the qualification of the students came by the teachers in various ways. And so of all the students that were accepted and all that were rejected, those that were rejected were put into a caste system. The only thing they had left for them was to grow up and inherit the parcel of land from their father's house or to have a suitable enough dowry to buy a husbandman so they would be taken care of for the rest of their life. And that was all there was to life. We could say they were the haves and the have-nots.

In the school itself there was a caste system that evolved naturally. We have it here in this school. The caste system is this: There are those who want it a little but are not willing to do a lot. There are those who want it more than a little and will match giving a little to get it; mostly they just buy it. Then there are those who passionately want it and will give anything to get it.

And "anything" does not mean the "things" but the ideal in which they have construed themselves to be: the beast, the image, the name, what does it represent, and indeed what does it stand for. Most of you don't even know what your names mean and no one cares. They just sound nice or noble, royal or pretty. You don't even know what their meaning is. So you are nameless, meaningless entities that do not have control over your life. The only control is that it is controlling you.

The students in the ancient schools were often groups within groups, and there were the sublime that mediocrity didn't even know existed. In the outer world that is how the caste system began and still exists to this day. The unfortunate entities that have been prejudiced against are not just the poor — because the poor will always be here, the poor have always been — and it is not just entities that don't come from noble houses. There are no noble houses any longer. It was the women, the girl children, but the most prejudiced-against being of all was the God within every human being.

Do you agree with this? I will tell you there is some truth in this, as bitter as it tastes, because you have a saying, "You can take the ass to water but you cannot make it drink." The father can give his child to the school but if the child does not want to give up his need to be a man of the world, to robustly experience himself in the world — or the woman give up the adulation she needs for her womanhood or to be possessed or possess that which counters and gives agreement to her existence — you cannot teach them anything because the place of surrender is not made to happen by your teacher. The teacher will take you to the initiation but who then becomes responsible for the initiation itself? The students themselves, for what they gain is all theirs and what they have lost, they have lost themselves. So how do you in the name of God endeavor to raise up a splendid few when the majority of them are of a rebellious house and don't care? There are people in this school that care to a degree, but only to a degree, in this only school of its kind in the world.

There are entities in the world, because of the nature of their lives, their programming, and their grid, that will never know God. They will never know the miraculous or the crumb from the table, and they haven't ever really wanted to either.

Christianity is a convenient religion to some degree. It allows the entity to have one entity dying for all of its sins, hanging on a cross forever, but there is a big trade-off in that. Yeshua ben Joseph reportedly was the only begotten son of God, so the rest of you measly bastards took the trade-off of not being sons and daughters of God. You were just left alone to live as long as you could have somebody to be sacrificed for you, and it wouldn't be you. It is a very convenient religion. It is also tyrannical. It has a mean and vicious God that it worships, and it says that the human being is born in corruption, lives in corruption, and by virtue of its own thoughts is a sinner, damned for all eternity.

That is a convenient religion because it puts you above your neighbor, and everyone here is competitive and likes being better than their neighbor. That is a sorrowful statement, sorrowful indeed. The truth is that there are very few people who have the devotion to become naked, to disillusionize everything in their life for the sake of knowing where those crumbs came from and being the administrator of larger ones. You could say, well, everyone should know this. No, because not everyone wants to know it.

The Journey of the Radical Few, the Revolution of Self

"I am talking about honorable, meaningful, enriched people of superb, mental excellence. And all of those attributes do not belong to the world; they belong to God and are reflected in the human being."
— *Ramtha*

Masters, there is a certain celebration that you should have inside of you. Let us look at this little extraordinary event. There are some of you that have had great manifestations. It is not what you get; it is the fact that you created it. It can be anything, as long as it manifests. That is the journey. If you have this ability, don't you find it awe-inspiring that you are here in this most macabre setting in front of a beautiful, mysterious teacher? Why you? When you look at how many people are alive in the world today, how many more will be alive tomorrow, is it that every group wants to think that they are indeed more special that they have the truth? Every group has the truth, don't they? The truth: There is not a universal truth; there is only individual truth. Let us look at this and take it one step further. You have experienced some miracles, extraordinary things. Most of the world out there has not experienced anything but faith. Faith, you could positively die on it and, of course, a lot do.

How wonderful are you? Extraordinary things are happening to you. Look at all the people in the world that need extraordinary things. Look at the hungry children that need an extraordinary miracle. Look at all the people who have not a home, and that has become a big issue now. They forgot they all used to be migratory animals, but now it is a big thing. Wouldn't it be wonderful if they had an extraordinary event?

How about all these people starving in the world and all that have the plague? Why don't they have an extraordinary thing happen to them? They all pray, at least most of them. Most people don't get on their knees and really start praying feverishly unless they get their tail in the wringer, and of course that is the appropriate time. I like that term "tail in the wringer" very much. Of course they pray and pray and pray and the child still dies in the mother's arms and flies are eating it up. I want to ask you something: Why do you have these extraordinary little miracles, and the very little miracles that you have would be acceptable to most starving, most diseased, prejudiced, humble, and pitiful people of the world?

Why are you getting them? Why do you deserve them when whole hosts of people pray for the misfortunate, and there is still misfortune? Could it be that you indeed do attend or belong — this term, belong, is a fickle term — to something that is extraordinary in itself? Yes. I want you to think about that and contemplate for a moment what you have received that is extraordinary that could have been utilized by a whole host of how many other people. I want you to think about why you. Immediately you start to feel guilty about your station. Some of you should feel guilty but most of you shouldn't. If you have had these experiences in this school, how many other places can do the same thing? They cannot.

What did it take for you to undergo the revolution of change in self? Look how long I have been hammering at you in how many different ways. It takes an entity who can say this: "There is something inside of me that responded to that name. It felt right."

Let's look at what you have undergone — me. How do you classify me: him or her, she, it, he, maybe? How did you classify me and the most notorious organization for a while that ever existed and all the things you had to do in order to be a part of the teachings? You know, it was different. There are a lot of reasons a long time ago why you shouldn't have come. They were obvious everywhere. Everything happened, planned to the "T," hated by the world, despised and envied by the religious organizations, despised by the ordinary citizens. Don't you understand that is what happens when anything is different? It filtered out straightaway those who would never make it to a point of thoughtful surrender, the student's journey to God. And you had to be tough enough, arduous enough, and diligent enough in order to even come here and be associated with me.

This is nothing to be ashamed of, nothing at all. And what are you learning from, a fraud?

Blessed be. How could a fraud teach you to miraculously manifest? Only that which would know it could teach it. So why you? Because you stepped out of the mainstream. And it wasn't faith that you had; it was a deep knowingness. Of all the runners I have sent to you, some of you have been brought to your knees, turned around, and blown away. It doesn't matter, I would do anything — I am not a moralistic entity — to carve the right people being at this place. The righteous have a right to be here because when it comes to surrendering to the Void, where these crumbs came from, you have to be willing to give it all up, disillusionize it all. You have to have that in you. The Ramtha people, as they are termed, are a radical few. The radical few have no intentions of overthrowing the government or the town. Who would want it? Leave to Caesar what is Caesar's, but what is God, you leave to yourself.

Becoming the radical few is the journey within the person to clarify and purify the entity to be a superbly moralistic person. I am talking about being honorable. I am not talking about robbers and highwaymen, which many of you have been. Remember the masters I told you about that you wouldn't recognize because some of them have their ears chewed off and scars on their face and countenance? They have been ruffians, but they are the ones that become the masters because they had the fire to make it. No one passive will ever make it, or one sitting on the fence, straddling it. I am talking about honorable, meaningful, enriched people of superb, mental excellence. And all of those attributes do not belong to the world; they belong to God and are reflected in the human being. That is the purpose of the human being, to reflect that place of sweet surrender and that the attitudes of the world become less and less and the focus on the God becomes more and more and more.

Do you understand the plan here, the prepa-ration for this entity's life, JZ Knight, the way this would all happen, the time it would happen in, and the human being it would happen with and why? The whole understanding suddenly becomes washed and clear because you had to have gone through this and kept that feeling alive regardless of the rebuking self-doubt so that it would remain supreme. And if you can go through that, then you can go through what it

takes to initiate a student into remarkable mas-
terhood. God isn't about lightbeings or whether
it is a man or a woman. God is, simply, and it is
consciousness that is lord and supreme. How
much more challenging could this be than to
have that appear through a woman? This prophecy is being fulfilled of old. It is astonishing that
a woman could be so bright, but a woman can
because its God can reflect through it. It takes
a lot of labor but it can happen. The teaching is
not about idol worshiping, is not about angels or
about Gods that live in far-off places. This teaching is not about worshiping the virginity of the
human being but its virtues. This is a teaching
rooted deep in consciousness as a ship whose
anchor is in the sky.

God is not about an image. It is about the
fathomless beauty, the formlessness of vibrant
life issuing forth from a human being. Regardless of the color of their skin, how young or old,
how fat or skinny, regardless of age, color, sex,
gender, or creed would never, ever determine
the power of God. Never has. This body is but
a garment in a vast closet. Look at me, this
beautiful, wise, eternal age, modern and contemporary body. It deceives the eyes but tam-

pers with the heart, and it is supposed to. Look at me. That which you love is coming through this mouth and through these eyes, radiating around this body, because everything I have taught you, I am.

The teaching is about formlessness; it is about consciousness. The initiations are to get you to a deeper level of surrender so that all of the trappings can go away and the eternalness of you can live on. This is what you came to learn. I am the only teacher you can talk to. As far as I know, Yeshua Ben Joseph hasn't answered any postcards and he doesn't want to.

That is why the miracles happen, because the truth is vitally alive in your midst. There is a fire in your midst and the flame is burning and is eternal. It represents the flame and the eternalness inside of you. It is a fool who can rebuke truth because of the way it looks, if it is male or female, or by its creed or color. That is a fool, and that fool deserves to die like all fools have always died. The glory of God knows no limitation. In your midst is a raging fire. It is the fires of initiation, the fires of a conscious truth that have provided the ways, the inlets, the rivulets to a conscious mind that has tapped the Source of eternal life.

You are the only people on the face of the Earth that have access to such a place in such numbers. Is that a safe God? It is its own natural, safe God. There are those of you who come here for the social aspect; you are going to church. There are others of you who come here that give a little, do a little, get a little. This is a place where the bounty of your abundance is only as great or small as your devotion to it — meaning becoming a formless being — and how much you apply yourself. So you see, it is naturally protected. The Source doesn't open up to fools and idiots and ne'er-do-wells. The fools don't even have the energy, the patience, the time, or desire to become greater than their station in life, which is in itself the creation of the caste system. The caste system is actually created by the people, so the kingdom of heaven doesn't have to worry about being robbed.

You know more and have been taught that which could never be written about and never explained. You have experienced more than any group of people alive today. If you want to test that, you are welcome to go out into the world, go to those mountains in the Far East and try to find something better or a different teacher and see if the miracles happen. They won't.

5. The Key Is Focus

*"Manifest for the love of the journey, not
for the thing itself but for the experience.
That and only that is what your God will
manifest for you through deep focus."*
— *Ramtha*

Creating reality is the simplest thing you will ever do because you have done it all your life. The way you have done it is you have grown up in a grid pattern that has caused a gridlock. The programs play day in and day out and always have. Changing to you only means giving up one heartache for another, going solitary, only regretting that you made the change. You never really change in the grid; you just emphasize some areas more than others. It is a game. You put the program in and it delivers what you can get in reality.

There are always the strings and the attachments and the pain because, remember, ninety percent of your memory is in lack. So why don't you take this pliable teaching with the key as focus? Why don't you take the key to the Void with you? Why don't you, in the surrender into nothingness, put the key in the lock and unlock truly an extraordinary change in your life, far-reaching and long-lasting?

If reality is that pliable that a whole host of students can work a field and be charmed and mystified by the way reality reacts and is quickened by thought, especially heightened thought, why don't you apply it every day? Why do you hold onto those dead mules that you drag behind you? Let the dead be gone, give them up. Why do you want to live as that little program? You can change, but you have to know what you want to change into, and what you want to change into is something other than the status quo, and that takes care of your entire program. That is the appropriate answer, because then in time those changes start to happen.

The deeper initiated you become, the more focused you become, the more powerful the manifestation and the quicker it comes, and on your terms. If you surrender to the Void and go there as a hot, sick lover, as a victim with sadness or sorrow in your heart, with guilt or hypocrisy — any of that slothfulness of the image, the beast — if you don't go to the Void naked, you will take to the Void your garments and you will manifest them a hundredfold.

For those of you who are having a lot of problems, this is your problem. The problem is that you like to have a problem. You like the drama; it makes you important. You can complain to people, they can feel sorry for you, you can solicit pity, and that is how you keep power running in your life, as small and meaningless as it is. You go to the Void looking for trouble. You may have a symbol that symbolizes freedom but you don't strip down when you go there. You go there polluted because you want to. You want to change but where you don't lose any of those contacts.

The purest people in the school can surrender it all, and have, and they are unassuming and brilliant. When I look at them, they are brilliant to me. They are unassuming and humble and intently wise. I know who they are and they stand out in all of you. They are sincere. They don't play games; they are just sincere. They are the makings of great people. There are others whose lights, their bands, pulsate and they are borderline. But what is wonderful about them is that they are growing and they are devoted, so at the next level of teachings they will completely comply.

Then there are others who want this more than anything, so they say, but are not willing to go the distance with it because this is how it must be: If you want to dine at the table of the Lord of Hosts, the King of Kings, if you are to dine at the head of the table of the Mother/Father Principle, indeed the Is, and dine there forevermore, eat the bread of life and drink the wine of life, then nothing in this life should be worth hanging onto.

That means that you go alone and you go naked, and that is the metaphor for surrendering into the Void and having this sense of total well-being but without an identity. It is not a sense of total well-being because you were hurting before you started, or this is an escape or you deserve it. It isn't qualified; it just is. It is a euphoric feeling of floating — floating. That is moving towards the table of God.

You can say, but I love my husband, I love blah-blah-blah. You need, need, need. If we were to draw a circle and put you in it and then put all the mirrors in that circle and have you name all the mirrors, that is who you are — the mirrors. Of course you couldn't give it up because that is you, and that is the image. Is it cruel to say, "Do I really have to give it all up in order to have something larger?" Let us qualify what giving it all up means. It means giving up the identity and all of its limitations that go with it. If it is important what people think about you, you are loaded with limitations. It is important that you convert the old, deep-rooted change to go back and comply with your friends. What you are is those mirrors, and that is what you must give up.

To go to God and dine at this table alone is sublime. But what would you not do to love greater, to love without condition deeply and richly? That is what you have to do, because there you can drink the wine of knowledge and wisdom, truth, you can eat the bread of eternal life, and this is what you bring back to those that are in your life. Does it mean that you have to throw everyone away? You have to break all of those mirrors. That is vitally important. How do you do that? By spending more time alone and in contemplation with no distraction.

People who have a problem being alone are people who live in the center of that sphere with all of its mirrors, because they don't like it unless you are there to report in, to tell you what you have been doing. You have to report. People who do not do this are having to hold together their identity, but those who start moving out of that are spending quality moments alone, contemplative, by yourself. I do not care how many children you have, how many wives, how many husbandmen, how many lovers, it does not matter. They are not worth you not knowing you. The more you do that, the greater your ability to surrender. But you can never go to God in that circle of mirrors ever, ever.

What are you alienating yourself against? You are alienating yourself against alienation. You are breaking the habit of limitations. That is what you are doing; that is all you are doing. The more the student does that, the more profound the initiations, the deeper they go and the more lasting they are. Everything I have ever done with you, for you, in your midst, and everything I have ever said to you, I have said and done and planned with extraordinary strategy, everything. I am not a fool.

I want to tell you that you have been trained in disciplines that work. But the discipline itself and the task that it must deliver, the prize, is to remove this image — bottom line, as you call it — to remove the thinking part, the endless chatter part of you to the solid yet expansive part of you that knows no boundaries. When focused on a singular thought, you have the etherical ability to become analogical, and that one thought starts to change in the human being's life that resurrects them from the living dead into eternal life.

This is the mystery: Why, if you know and have been taught this, do you not use it? If you do not use it, every day of your life will manifest accordingly. For those that are partially awake, partially have an awakened day, but for the most part are unconscious or asleep. Why do you not use this tool that became such a powerful witness in the field or in the mystic dance? Are you so prejudiced against your God? Are you so staunch and even stoic in your resistance because you think this is washing your brains? Let me tell you, those who criticize that this is brainwashing, their greatest fear is correct, because it is. What happens when you wash anything that is dirty? It becomes clean.

Are you determined to live your life as victims of your past? How long will you play this game? And when will you rise up above the murk and the mire and surrender to something that can make it all change? If reality is so pliable and so magical as it has been in the extraordinary little miracles in your life, why don't you use it? Furthermore, why don't you allow your thinking mind to be put asunder? Why don't you surrender to the moment of nothingness?

Let me tell you something which is very wise information. Those who still are in want, who are still perjurers to their own truths, those who will not utilize the gift that has been given to them deserve their station in life, their lack, fully and righteously deserve their habits and their own limitations. Ignorance is excusable. Philosophy, to have a philosophical opinion, that is even excusable. You can have a philosophy about the way things are and that is really only an opinion because that is what philosophy means. It is not scientific, doesn't duplicate itself, nor does it lend itself to dimensional inspection. Philosophies are safe. We can even excuse personal ignorance because of a philosophy. But you cannot excuse downright lethargy and wallowing in the pigsty from which you have so arduously preached and desired liberation once you know the method, the secret.

Why is this the truth? If you had the extraordinary experiences — and the experiences were a direct result of the knowledge and the training and the tests that you have thus far engaged in this school — then you have the truth to all reality. If you haven't used it, you deserve exactly the kind of life you insist upon having.

What did I just do? I called your bluff. You cannot sit there any longer and say, "Well, nothing is happening in my life but I try so hard." Bull. You try so hard not to try. That is all you do. And you whiners and you endless wanters, you want the next teaching, the next level of experience because you are bored with this one. You haven't made it work for you because you didn't want it working for you. You want a reason to be a part of something, and there is this cold chill in the back of your mind that raises the hair on the back of your neck and says, "This might be the truth."

You want to live when all hell breaks loose in the days to come, when one fine morn things are different. You want to be where it is safe but you are not really committed. You want the next teaching so you have a reason to stay here when you haven't even mastered the ones that I have given you. So is there a caste system in this school? There most certainly is, and it is the self-elected that have created it. There are the victims, the endless victims, and they will always be in this school until they reach about the fifth year, and in the fifth year they will be no more.

If anything is worth loving, these teachings are, most certainly. Philosophically they are beautiful, unlimited, flawless. To any seeker who likes seeking, to any person who likes arguing, to any entity who likes to visualize the horizon without ever experiencing it, these are the most beautiful teachings in the entire world. They are about a God that is faceless and formless that has always loved you but has no problem getting rid of you. It is about a God who would give you everything you ever wanted if only you would become self-aware. It is about that you have never been judged right or wrong but for the sake of personal evolution, for the gaining of wisdom. It is about that every human being has the inalienable right to wonder, even contemplate, about the kingdom of heaven, and that there was no one, personal

God but that all are Gods.

And if this be true then indeed you must be divine. But man and woman by their own earnest efforts create divinity as an external reflection; otherwise it always remains philosophical. These are the most beautiful teachings in the world, they truly are. There is a reason to come here and bring your children because they will grow in equality and perhaps, through them, will do what you never did, the daring to become that which was always without form. There are going to be some of you who are not going to be able to go to extraordinary levels because you have the truth and you insist on living in the idea — not the standard but the idea — of lack and punishment and tyrants and victims, and you are intent upon destroying your bodies. You have your own caste system.

You are going to change it. Furthermore, you have the gift of knowledge and a fire in your midst that can initiate you, a hierophant. Not one of you is a hierophant. I am a hierophant. You have been given a truth in the beginning that can manifest something out of nothing. You have the power to create a whole new life, in fact a whole different identity, to be certain.

And the reason the people ahead of you haven't is because they cling to their identity. Do not idealize them. Let the fire burn in you. Let it be your fire, your devotion. Put no one before you and look up to your God only.

Why doesn't this little ray of hope, these fragments from a greater table, go to the starving people in other lands and here at home? Why doesn't this crumb go to the desperately ill, the hard workers for humanity who, God knows, need a lighter load? Has it occurred to you that the whole world could use this information, and what you are doing — taken for granted — has been a calling that you responded to but have fallen into lethargy? I want you to honor what you have been taught. Love it as a philosophy or treasure it as a truth, whichever one is correct for you.

The ideal of this school was not to create saviors but to create living Christs. A Christ is a contemporary word. The translation that is more correct is the "One Being." Christos is a sanctified word meaning the unknown fully manifested through the known, God/man realized, indeed God/woman realized. It means the unknown fully realized through the instrument

of the known. The idea here is to take ignorance, to take on humanity who are outrageous
enough to have responded to such a call and
have what it takes to go through a school that
has no duplicate — it cannot be compared with
anything else — and be able to stand alone in
that school.

However, having what it takes and having the will and desire, that I cannot give you.
This school is to create God — the unknown
manifested through the knowns — in a multiple
situation, not in just one human being, not even
five or twelve, the holy number, but in a host
of people.

There are a lot of entities that belong to
this school but very few by comparison with
the entire world. Can you imagine what your
seventh-year initiation would be like, your
seventh- year training, and would it entail the
world? It absolutely does. I am not training you
to go home; I am training you to manifest it,
that one day the truth is preserved in qualified,
deeply enriched, conscious beings. So, you see,
your small-mindedness and that little game you
play one day could affect all those people that
are dying in the world, because you received

the crumb and got the schooling and had the fire. Perhaps their genetic deliverance will be through a being such as yourself. How great must you be to stand in the midst of hollowed death, to stand in the midst of filth and stench and oozing sores and hollowed eyes and dung and crusted limbs and swollen bladders? How great are you going to have to be? How naked are you going to have to be of your own personal wrath, your indignation, your personal limitations, and personal needs? They will not exist. The man who rides the horses will be able to tender the world. What is the greater destiny? The whole world, of course, because you don't give a man food on his plate to fill his belly; you give him the seeds that he can plant and teach him how to feed his own belly. The crumbs do not fall to the profane. They fall to the outrageous, radical few whose ultimate destiny is to liberate the world from its own ignorance.

Why haven't you changed and been the lord of your days; too tired? Why haven't you been the lord of your body; too weak? Why haven't you fulfilled the idea of lack? Do you like to suffer? And who are you living for, the image in the mirror of all those people in your life that you report to, or are you willing to change in spite of them and the whole world and become naked? Since you are worthy of eternal life, why do you insist upon going without and playing the game of lack; too lazy? Is the world too hard on you? Is work too arduous? Maybe that is what you need. Apply what I have endeavored to teach you in so many ways and watch its majesty work and be caught up in the awe of the journey. Things will become incidental.

Manifest for the love of the journey, not for the thing itself but for the experience. That and only that is what your God will manifest for you through deep focus.

The key is focus — no thinking, a stilled mind — and that is the key.

6. The Secret of "I Am," Knowingness, and Long, Timeless Thoughts

"A long thought does not encumber an entity with the tedium of a singular thought but blesses the entity by becoming that thought."
— *Ramtha*

Let us start by looking at extraordinary things. Where can we find extraordinary, theoretical things in the supermarket of the Void — extra-ordinary or ordinary? If it happens to you, it means it is known but has never been your experience so let's call it memory. Ninety percent of the personality of the brain is memory and its charge is negative, which means it is in lack. It is the modus operandi of the image. So anything ordinary can be identified straightaway because it is in memory, but it doesn't necessarily mean it has been your experience.

All these extraordinary things have been a part of identifiable memory but never personal experience. You can start by desiring the crack to get wider by going to a deeper place

and taking with you a focused thing into surrender or perhaps just going to this place and
surrendering and seeing how to do that. The
word abstract still denotes form; it is unemo-
tional. Let's not use the word abstract and go
to another word, formless. In order to define
the word formless, we must have its contrary,
which is form.

How you see yourself is going to be a difficult task because most of you never see yourself.
Formless is the opposite of form, so perhaps the
experience is to see how much deeper you can
go and how surrendered you can become so that
all you are is "I am." I am not formless, because
if you say that, it means you are coming from
form, to deny it. I am. I am just "I am," and see
how you float, how naked and deep you can go.
But victims, beware. If you take the victim with
you, you are going to get hellfire in the morning.
Strip it down and blow it away and do not go as
the victim, the identity, or the persecuting habit.
Go as naked as you can. Strip the layers away,
falling backwards, ripping it away from you,
until you just are. Stay there, know this place,
because this is the place and the garment that
you wear when you come to dine with the Lord

of Hosts. And the next day and the next day — it doesn't have to be every day — this should be as natural as breathing, that the focused mind simply creates with a single thought.

Faith is a very emphasized word in world religions. Faith healing, you have lost the meaning of what that means. It shouldn't be faith; it is called knowingness, and it is so absolute that it isn't even an argument. Know, know, know "I am." Know when it is created, it is. Know, and it is an immutable law. And when you are that powerful, you have nothing that challenges it; not even the image would dare to challenge it. The roots into the Void and the pillars to heaven are knowingness. That is what I want you to experience. And when you create, don't you mealy-mouth your creation; know that it is. If you don't know it, by God you get to where you know it. You know it and it is. It is immutable, and none shall put you under and take it from you. The only one that would ever take it from you would be your own game-playing self that has undermined it and been prejudiced against any that would liberate you from your own preferred enslavement.

You have some options. They are very

kind. The next levels of initiation will be for the truly sincere people. I have taught some of you the power breath to the Void, how to create a three-dimensional thing. You needed to have something to create there because you could ask, how would I know I am in the Void? You are looking for something to tell you, and the thing, if it is identifiable, is not the Void. How do you know you are in the Void when you are having to search for something to tell you that you are there and it is no thing? It is midnight blue. It is behind your eyes. It is deep inside you too. It is sublime, timeless thought. You can go there, you can make a card, you can dance. Perhaps you would like to do all three: the power breath, go to the Void, and the power dance.

You have some options, from all that I have told you, to make some changes. If I were you, and of course I am not, I would start, since I know you are bluffing. I know your game, and you can't ask me for help any longer because you are going to have to do it yourself. I would start cracking the grid. I would start practicing stripping down for the Void. I would do it not because you have to — dragging you kicking and screaming to the Void is no fun for me or you — but because you see you have a new lease on eternity now. You really do understand why you are here and they are there and that perhaps your beingness is much more important than you ever thought before.

You can strip it all the way down. And whatever you do, however you do it, the way that I have taught you, you go to a formless state. Here are the signs: floating, lightness of being, and a delightful lucidity about just being. That is when you will know.

A blessed entity is defined as one who is loved, whose life is enhanced in spite of its image by its God. A blessing is the interference of your God to the demands of your image. It is an entity who possesses the extraordinary ability to have a long thought. And when it is said unto you — traveler on your path — "indeed may your days be blessed with long thought," long thought is that singular focus, that singular thought that can wind deep into the night until early morn. A long thought can traverse the skies all day long and meet the rising moon, and see it wax and wane all the way through dawn. A long thought does not encumber an entity with the tedium of a singular thought but blesses the entity by becoming that thought.

An impatient mind is a young mind. Wisdom is defined not by age but the wondrous ability for long thoughts. If your God interrupts your lifestyle — if your God breaks up your relationship, if in the name of your God your life turns topsy-turvy, if you have changed and no one understands or even likes you, if you smell different, look different — you can blame it on God, for to be blessed by your God is an interruption of this boring, boring life. Masters are noted for their long thought, piercing eyes that see through and through, and their wild Spirit cannot be captured or owned, just adored and bitterly respected.

My beautiful people, you have been chosen and perhaps you are special, for you have received a modicum of blessing, as perhaps a niblet or tidbit of a noncholesterol snack leads to a greater feast.

Isn't it about your hour? Isn't it your coming-out? Shouldn't it be your début? Stop feeling sorry for yourself, abandoned and alone, picked on and abused. Throw it all away and wake up in the early morn with a new fire and new attitude to create the day that can be called, at day's end, the creation of a God that has been indeed well lived.

Grow up. Lacks are outdated in the school. God does not manifest gold unless it is for a reason, and the only reason is an experience you never had before. God manifests clarity and genius not for the sake of adoration but for the experience. You are here to be happy, whether you like it or not.

Crumbs from a Divine Table

"There are no other teachings like these teachings. They are so beautiful because they uplift the lowly human being to a status of divinity. Instead of seeing the wretchedness inside the human being, God is always seen."
— *Ramtha*

I have taught my students the most sacred knowledge, the most freeing knowledge. They have gained the wisdom and indeed an experience.

My students have had crumbs from God's table and the crumbs fell purposely, as if it were a carrot in front of the rabbit's nose. But when it came to the largest schemes in life, they doubted or perhaps didn't want to resolve the dilemmas that they were in. Don't you find that curious? It is also interesting to know that the image has an image to uphold, and if a person has been a victim all their life, it is the only way they have ever known how to express. Victims do not want miracles. They want pity and compassion, which is supposed to stimulate love but it never really does. It is also what causes sickness and illness because that further stimulates compassion but that doesn't last very long either.

This is the only organization in the world that has the truth. Well, there is no such thing as "the truth." Truth is a personalized phenomenon. There isn't "the" truth; there is only evolution. If you had an opportunity to look at every organization in the world, surely you would say this stands alone, because in what other organizations is God readily accessible to miraculous happenings than this one? This is the only one. This is the only gathering and school of its kind where it works. My God, it works.

Are these the true teachings? Absolutely, but they are only philosophy to most of you.

They are philosophical, deeply beautiful, and absolutely freeing to the human being. There are no other teachings like these teachings. Everything else is stained and colored. They are so beautiful because they uplift the lowly human being to a status of divinity. Instead of seeing the wretchedness inside the human being, God is always seen. Human potential is not limited by its peers or its society. It knows no boundaries because God doesn't know any boundaries, never did. You can raise your children in these teachings that teach human morality — not sexual morality but human morality — and justifiable self-honor.

Philosophically they are superb, but the master is here to learn to be a master, not a philosopher. They are learning to personalize every teaching, so hence the school is here to bring forth knowledge and then, as a hierophant, to force the student through the knowledge as a total experience. Then the student can say, "I have tasted of the crumbs of a divine table." And if they are hungry, they are going to want it all and, to their delirious shock, will find it is the simplest thing they have ever done. The most difficult thing — the most difficult — is getting over their programming.

I leave you with that truth and with blessings from your God of long thoughts, creative days, and change. So be it.

Prayer for Change

O Mysterious One,
what else call I you?
Nameless one.
O being of wonder,
I have struggled
in the midst of my doubt.
I am short-spirited
and heavy mass.
But, O Mysterious One,
enlighten me,
move through me
to be that immutable
life that I long for.
O nameless one,
open me up this night.
This I desire
from the Lord God
of my being.
So be it.
To life.

7. Initiation at Paradise Beach

"After three days and nights of sincere focus, holding it, then the Spirit of the entity is tested. The sincerity is tested, the image is broken asunder, and it is an earnest man or woman who walks off Paradise Beach."

— Ramtha

If you have had a small miracle happen, why not devote the time to put the key in the lock and unbolt the door to fantastic realism? I observed three people in the state of commerce today. They were trying to calculate how long it would take them to pay off a certain item. To "pay off" is an interesting statement because it means that you are getting something but it will own you from here on out until you are free of its bondage. You may have to have it just for the sake of living, but living has become bondage in itself. I watched them, and it would take approximately thirty years on this one particular thing. Thirty years; that is a long time for you, isn't it?

I watched them struggle between sovereignty and survival. The second person that I watched had a companion and they were looking at purchasing an automachine, and the automachine had installments to be paid. They were also figuring out how many years of their life this was going to take, and it turned out it would take twenty-four months. These were advanced students. Not once had they applied what they learned in the great school, not once, because the very thought of even sitting for three days and nights was too long. They got bored thinking about it, their image went crazy, but they would work thirty years instead — thirty years.

My beautiful little initiation called Paradise Beach has everything that a resort place could ask for — heat. It is wonderful, a wonderful place to go. The initiation had to do with sitting still and riding those great "horses" in your head, in which the students became masters. Now this is laughable. They had to become masters over all of those horses. The "horses" ran over them, plowed them into the ground. It was a carnage at Paradise Beach. I laughed and laughed and laughed alone. It was actually my first initiation of an advanced group.

Let me sum up what this advanced master would say if I said this to them: "Master, come to Paradise Beach. I will reinstruct you in the art of a long thought and the blessedness of possessing such a thought and how to move it into the subterranean layers of the Void. Now there is a price you must pay. The price is you can't move, can't talk, can't hear, can't eat, you must fast and sit perfectly still, sitting up for three days and three nights. If you do that, you will have your hovel; it will manifest itself. An opportunity will present itself because — let's talk turkey — God, your God of course, the nameless one, is interested in striking deals but the deals have a little catch. Don't ask it for money or it will fry you. Don't ask it for something you already have or it will take it away from you. Ask for something you have never had."

And you strike a bargain. You say, "O Mysterious One, I most desperately need a hovel, indeed I need a place that I can become self-sufficient until I know better, until I have gained all the wisdom that I need to know. I am willing to do whatever is necessary for me to have this. So whatever experience I have never had for the sake of internalizing wisdom so that you and I can live happily ever after together, then send me this experience that the result of the little prize would be my home. But send me a grand adventure in getting it."

And God, that wise entity, says, "Indeed."

After three days and nights of sincere focus, holding it, then the Spirit of the entity is tested. The sincerity is tested, the image is broken asunder, and it is an earnest man or woman who walks off Paradise Beach.

If I said to this entity, "Do this but, mind you, you cannot go to sleep," he will take the thirty-year loan, thirty years. Why do you suppose that is? If I said to a wretchedly poor mother and her starving infant at her collapsed bosom, "Come, sit with your child for three days and nights and focus only on the things you need," she would focus on food. And she would stay there three days and three nights, and she would have her food. She would have it. Why isn't she here instead of you who would rather take the thirty-year loan?

Perhaps it is the definition of miracle. A miracle is something that God gives you "just because." You didn't really have to do anything; it sort of happened incidental to you. This is also categorized as being lucky; correct? Perhaps it is a definition in your memory. Miracles, you don't have to do anything to get them. If you are a religious person, you would, however. You would have to pray endlessly and prostrate yourself, forgive everyone in your life, ask God's forgiveness, lie and eat dirt, wear sackcloth and ash, fast and do all of that and somehow, miraculously, it sometimes happens to those people. It is no wonder; they had their own Focus Beach.

Somewhere in your metaphysical training, for what that is worth, someone told you that the Source will provide, that the universe provides, for your needs. But no one ever finished the story because they were afraid to finish it, for then no one would listen to them. The universe, the cosmos, will provide all the things that you need, provided of course that you execute the procedure of in-depth, conscious focus, which means that you desire the experience. And of course now we are moving into a vague, gray area. Is it an intentional manifestation or is it a miracle? It depends. If you focus long enough on it, it really wouldn't be a miracle; it would be the result of consciousness and energy intentionally and willfully engaged. If it were a miracle, it may have seemed that in the beginning because to your wonderful delight, it works. In spite of yourself, it works. So that is the miracle. My God, you are wretched and awful, you smell bad and are guilty, and you have done all these things all of your life, but it worked. You never thought you could do anything — well, heaven's host, start singing.

So the first one was a miracle; the second one was a flop because then you started worrying if you could do it again. Let me tell you, the man would not take three days and nights in focus because he doesn't really want it that much. So he would take thirty years and a long time to decide if he ever really wanted it rather than to take three days and nights out of his life and intently create it. The house or hovel is incidental. It was the experience that wrought the adventure that brought it into manifestation. If you do not have adventure in your life in which you instrumentally participate and are also the instrument in manifesting, then no matter what you get will not have any worth to it. So for thirty years he will be tied up and labor to pay for his hovel.

Here is something else that is important. You can accept crumbs from the table of God but you doubt very seriously if you can take the whole feast because you are not that clean, that pure, and that naked yet. Is it in fact something about the way you must be taught that you get these extraordinary miracles in increments of small little things which are acceptable, instead of large things which are deniable? Could it be there was something inside of him told him that the whole time focusing out there for three days and nights that he would never believe it because he could never accept something that large? This is an image consciousness, to be certain, because this image consciousness has measured large versus small. Small, it can accept; large, it can't. A dimensional mind — a mind that measures everything but is one that has dominion over it — can get everything it wants. It is not about the thing itself, whereas the image thinks only of the thing itself. The God says, "It is the experience, indeed it is the journey."

I want to ask you an important question: How strong is your desire to go naked in a focus, to become so un-image, so un-male, unfemale, un-troubled, with a lightness of being? How close are you to doing that compared with your standards of acceptability? What will you really accept that you can create and what you really can't?

Those entities that ended up with the twenty-four month deal, let me tell you what happened with that little story. The one entity really wanted to go contemplate out in nature about this. The deal was postponed so that one sincerely could contemplate in focus and the other one regrettably left it alone. Which one do you think is going to pull it through: the one regretting, passing up the deal, or the one who goes and focuses? They walked away from an opportunity to have it today because the one wanted to go focus. That is a powerful will. In the light of temptation it says, "No, I want to go focus on this." Something in it is saying, "This is temptation. Move away from this. Come to me, be still, know that I am God. Let us commune over this." And in focus, God is the instrument. The whole reason for God is the purpose of focus and rejuvenation and creation. That is a powerful master, and it was a woman. The woman will have her desire without signing anything. She will have an experience that will provide it as a bonus.

Miracles are those items in which you do not have an absolute knowingness that you can tackle and bring into the world. You don't have to know how they are brought into the world or into your life. You just have to focus on them, because if you start trying to tie things together and figure it all out, you are going to limit its construction. It will have to be contracted to fit into your grid, and there is no room for miracles in the grid. There are those of you who consider the miraculous is that which you doubt could occur to you with every fiber in your being. That is a miracle.

Knowingness is the ability to focus and manifest anything — anything — because the thing itself is incidental. Your God is interested in the experience. It wants the wisdom, to eternalize you forever and ever and ever. That is what it wants. It could care less about this little object because it can raise its frequency and take it back to nothingness. Its value is nothing but the journey of it is everything. The entities who become very wealthy as masters, their wealth becomes incidental to them; it becomes as a result of them. But their great treasure is not in the things they possess but their powerful consciousness because they only have to focus their mind in any one direction, and it is. They have learned an immutable wisdom: Don't figure out how it is going to come and don't plan it. It will happen because it is an experience, an adventure, that you need to have, and they are willing.

Why are you here? Why you instead of someone who really would sit here and be impassioned to save their life or their children or improve their status of living if they had the keys? You know, there is a certain point to where Christianity becomes a farce in the face of starvation. Melt down those golden crosses and chalices and buy food. Someone who is hungry in their belly will labor for their next meal, and it will be a sincere labor, a worthwhile labor. A person who is hungry in Spirit will also labor. They are the devoted ones that are deeply devoted to what they call their personal truth and the journey of knowledge in evolution. It is their journey and they are equally hungry.

Those are the ones who went through this initiation and became changed people as a result of it because they were hungry. So how hungry are you? How much do you want to change and are you afraid of it? Are you afraid to give up your victimization because who would you be unless you didn't have a past? Are you afraid to give up your habits because then what would keep you alive, because you are dead? Surrendering to your God to become naked.

If you say to a master, "Master, what is your greatest desire?"

"My desire is to always be filled with desire."

Now you have a key that fits into a lock. What can't you do? You can do anything — anything. The world is your oyster, so is the cosmos. You are only going to get what is equal to your desirability, your hunger, your passion, your devotion, your sincerity. And it may be a feeble amount that will manifest another crumb, but the crumb represents a massive banquet, a feast of a thousand years that waits for those who can come to the table naked, not without the garments on their body but naked as a consciousness. It is where the consciousness is not Harry or Joe or George or Alice or May, but the consciousness is without habit, without corruption. Its memory is being turned into wisdom.

It is rich in experience and there is no lack in it.

That is the entity that goes to the table where these crumbs fell from the Void. Only a naked entity can move as a formless being beyond the veils to know the glory of God. An image never would, because when you ask the question, "What is the Void, what am I supposed to see?" don't you understand the foolishness of the question? You don't see anything. Here is where you see; there is where you be. And beingness is formlessness and without structure, without limits, and without bounds.

Doesn't it make sense to you that if you could be a beingness, a formlessness, that you would know no boundaries? And then if you had the ability of long thought and you took a long thought into a state of beingness, that nothing else existed save the long thought and you, that the thought would become absolute reality? Yes. Absolute reality.

You are here because I called you here. You have enough rebel and outrageousness in you to come and learn under that which you have never seen and yet is more alive, more deeply desirable than any human being you know. I called you to come and learn to be what I am, not myself but what I am, a consciousness that in any vehicle that it manifests through, its glory is absolute. Just because I am no longer seven feet tall, have cinnamon-colored skin, black dancing eyes, long fingers and swift arms does not lessen the caliber of my beingness.

I am here so you could come and see that God is a woman, a blessed woman, that God is also a man, a blessed man. When you can come and listen and see the miraculous results of the learning, then you have enough rebel and highwayman in you that this is where you belong. The truth is so outrageous because it is obvious. That is its outrageous nature and that is why you are here. You would be bored anywhere else.

In a true initiation, a deep initiation, the students themselves must make the commitment. You can sit still, suffer, count time, and go to sleep or you can sit still, become lucidly conscious, and move into a realm of formless thought and then want more and more and more, falling down a well shaft into a glorious mind, drinking the drought of a mystical river. You can do that too. Some did that and are changed forever.

For those of you that haven't had that experience, you are gaining a wisdom on the heels of those who have. You are here to take those crumbs and get hungry because they are in your life. You are also here to learn devotion, not an enslavement but a devotion that says you surrender to the knowledge, surrender to the test. And that is when the master is born because the master conquers not the knowledge or the tests but the limitations that prohibit the truth from becoming their reality.

The master does not want to know psychology, philosophy; it wants to know truth. So it will grasp at the wisp, the gossamer threads of philosophy, and shred it apart until it has consumed every thread of philosophy and has become a living truth.

8. The Greatest Conquest
of All — Yourself

*"In the mastery of the beast, the warrior
inside of you rises up in spite of your lack
and does it anyway. That is what slays the
dragon. Blow after blow after blow, one
day you will cut its head off. And when the
head is cut off, you are a free human being
to soar with eagles, dance in the sun, know
the other side of the moon, and go into
another dimension."*

— Ramtha

Everything here works. Every teaching, every experience works. If I were you, I would make this the most important thing in my life because it is like saying, "You can have three wishes from the genie or you will be the genie." And of course if you are the genie, you are going to change color — green. You may not like green; it may not look good with your wardrobe. But green it is, if you are going to be the dispenser of all wishes. In surrender, it is nothing to come to the table of God and eat bountifully.

If I were you, I would become very devoted, and the first thing I would do is listen to everything I say, of course. The next thing is do everything I say. Every now and then I will give you options and you are to select one of them.

The third thing would be to find this hunger inside of you, find out why I called you here. What is it that you possess, that truly humble people of the world should know but cannot know? What is it in you that has made you come here to the only place of its kind? There are imitators, I tell you, everywhere but they don't have the truth. You have it here, because it is born inside of you. Find out do you have the capacity, regardless of your highwayman past, your rebel, your rebellious house? Regardless of your past, do you have what it takes as a distant warrior to perhaps conquer the greatest conquest of all, yourself, and the self is the beast inside of you? And the beast is the grid. It is the boxes that hold, separated and divided, consciousness and energy forms. It only knows what it knows and rejects everything else. The only miracles that could have ever occurred in your house could have been extraordinary-ordinary, because they are in your memory — but out of the predictable — thus making them a miracle.

That is the beast in you, the demon, the ugly one, the underminer, the one that told this beautiful man today that he would rather go thirty years in hard labor than focus for three days and nights because he asked his image whether he could do it. What did you think it would say? "No." That is the beast, the dragon you have to conquer. That is brilliantly tied in with everything you are going to learn in my school. Listening right now, the beast is heavy on you because when I ask you to do something, you have to drag yourself to do it. It has been undermining you the entire time you are listening to me.

In the mastery of the beast, the warrior inside of you rises up in spite of your lack and does it anyway. That is what slays the dragon. Blow after blow after blow, one day you will cut its head off. And when the head is cut off, you are a free human being to soar with eagles, dance in the sun, know the other side of the moon, and go into another dimension, to come with me and let me take you places. To be a free entity of the beast is this, this ultimate enslaver. You cannot argue; you are a fool if you say that the teachings do not work, because they do. Consciousness and energy indeed manifests reality and the insult is growing more and more every time we meet. The fact the teachings work is immutable proof it is no longer philosophy; it is.

To become a warrior with a great sword in the right hand and a ball and chain in the left is freeing your internment. That is the master that is looking straight ahead. It doesn't look back, doesn't look here or there; it is looking straight ahead. It is focused. So every moment I have you do something and you get up and do it, there is a great broadsword that takes another slice into the walls of the image where the dragon lives in its lair. Every moment that you get up and are greater than your body, greater than your fatigue, your hunger, your discomfort, every moment that you build something that is unusual inside of you, you are putting the dragon asunder. And the master masters this all the days that he or she is a master until the head of the dragon is lopped off and the crown of Christ is realized. God then freely flows through the garment of the human body so God is within your midst, truly — not tainted, not boxed in, but walks amongst you unaware.

It is possible for an incredible mind to exist in a human body. It is possible for that which created the cosmos to be a human being. Why not? It created it. If I were you, I would determine if you really want to be here because you are going to have to get used to the classroom extending outside of the classroom, the field extending outside of the field. The next time you wake up, which we hope is tomorrow morning, instead of waking up and being heavy in the day, wake up before the sun rises and focus on the day. Take a long thought, with the training, and make that day joyful — joyful — because if you focus it, it will be, and this beast is put asunder and with that comes a lightness of being and a freedom.

If you want to be here in this school, you are going to have to get used to stop being a victim because it doesn't wash here any longer. I don't care what your problem is, it is your problem. You created it; you can uncreate it. You are the one that holds it in line. I don't care what your habits are, they are chains to you. I don't care how pitiful you feel, you are just a wretched little tyrant. Stop it; you don't have to feel that way. Shock everyone and change. You have the power to move mountains, the power to bring into your life anything you want, except you are going to have to remember that your partner in this will not give you anything because your focus is the long focus to the Void, taking with you a thought to the altar, to the bosom of God. You are going to have to say, "I want the journey. I desire this journey."

If you are a "things" person, you are not going to get the things. You are going to become a victim very quickly and you are going to live in a lot of lack. If you desire the experience, you will have many adventures and the things will collect and will become incidental. The hunger is for the next adventure, the next challenge, the next manifestation that challenges everything you have learned to date. Start focusing, start blowing, start dancing like a pagan who understood the power of the dance. Do it not because you just want to dance but for what it produces in the human being and use your training. Don't make this into church; don't come to school on Sunday. Don't dress up and come here and socialize. I have people that can replace you. Come here because what you gain is changing your life, that there will be no disconnection between the two. Manifest in your life, for God's sake. Stop being victimized. Stop being in lack. Wake up in the morning and create the day instead of being enslaved by it. And if it isn't working out, if it isn't happening, I will tell you what to look for: an undermining, and the undermining is self-doubt. The undermining is you don't really want it. The undermining is that you don't want to have to change if you get it. And if all of those are in effect, decide if you really want it after all. Once you understand what is undermining you, you can blow them away and it will manifest straightaway.

And, last, if I were you, not only would I see life as the practice hall of the school but everything I learn, I would apply all day long. And the more you apply it, the happier you are going to get. If I were you, I would have wonderful, slumbering nights and my dreams would be wild and magical just like my days. And if I were you, I would start calling myself a master and living up to it. So be it.

The Three Primordial Principles and How to Put Them into Action Outside of Time

"Now you begin to understand the importance of desiring to unify with a Void that is not bound or measurable by structure because it has no limitations. God, however you want to call it, must be formless, it must be no thing, it must be the absence of familiarities, it must have the absence of memory because it is the absence of time."

— Ramtha

Consciousness and energy creates the nature — nature — of reality. How did all of this get here? Through seeds of evolution. All of this came from some beginning point of thoughtful awareness. If you were going to create something, is the act of creation unusual? Is it indigenous in you or is it something you must learn? It is indigenous in you.

The original mandate to your God was to make known the unknown. Make known the unknown out of what? One vast nothing materially, all things potentially. So number one — consciousness and energy creates the nature of reality — answers the question, what are you? You are consciousness and energy creating the nature of reality, which is life. What is your modus operandi? Number two, to make known the unknown. Out of what? Number three, nothing.

If the modus operandi is to make known the unknown, then why are you continuously living the known? Habit, the broken records. Habit is actually the threads of the grid. It is habit that locks in consciousness and energy into little grooves. The consciousness determines what the energy will be: anger, repulsiveness, envy, love, jealousy, hate, wantonness, hypocrisy, all of those human emotions.

You are in school to find out who you are, why you are here, and for what reason. I do believe we have answered all three of those in the first three sentences above. If it is that simple, then what is the procedure involved and what are the procedures to exercise the mandate? Since you already are what you are, number one, the procedure to access the mandate, number two, is this: Consciousness and

144

energy originally created the dream and then reflected it back, engaged it, and then got wisdom. This consciousness and energy was then fulfilling the law of making known the unknown, and the wisdom is the jewel of the experience.

As wisdom begins to coagulate in numbers it defines you as an eternal being. To say that a person is infinitely wise is quite an outrageous statement. It means that the human being is all wisdom, that every experience in their life was no longer memory or habit but became virtue, wisdom. All of those pearls of wisdom are what will make that entity live forever because they are embossed on this timeless element — God. The wiser the human being is, the greater the option for an eternalized existence, which is also fulfilling the mandate.

You make known the unknown for the experience, not the habit. If there were any pill for eternal life, wisdom is the pill but the action is experience. We have a small dilemma here because we are going to have to break down the walls of the grid in order to release enough energy that will allow you to go on this adventure because otherwise you usually undermined it yourself.

Let's come back to make known the unknown. We have a safeguard where I come from, and the safeguard is you couldn't possibly think of a way to get where I am because you are terrified of the unknown. Unless it is shaped like something that you can identify, you are not going to create it so you continue to create things that are ordinary.

Think about this for a moment. Where would you get the thought to define dimensional reality? What part of your grid has that information? If you have to form a thought, that is where it comes from, your grid. So you are not getting anything new; you are just getting recycled ignorance. You don't even know the questions to ask. It is an embarrassment but it is the truth. This is a little bit of a dilemma because the only thing that you know is ninety-percent memory, which is theoretical. It means that the brain has memorized it but you have never experienced it so you are empty. And all of that ninety percent is negative. It is geared to lack, not abundance. Memory is a state of lack because memory is only part of the equation. Memory is to focus on it so you can experience it.

How do you make known the unknown?

With what tool would you make it? Where are you going to get the thought to have an unknown experience and what kind of thought would it be? If it is a square thought, then it is not unknown; it is known. If it is a loving thought, that is not unknown; that is known. How about if it is a vision through a garden? That is not unknown; that is known. How about if you visualize yourself being a master in long robes? Oh, that is yesterday's news. You have already had that fantasy. That is why you are here; correct?

What thought would be used to make known the unknown? What are you going to do? Focus on the unknown. That is a swell answer. How are you going to do this? We are really in a pickle barrel, aren't we? My God, you want to evolve but where is the stuff of evolution? And if you are supposed to come up with it, we are going to come up in short order, to be certain.

Focus on the Void because in the Void all things are potentials. Focus on nothing. How do you do that? By just doing it, just doing it. If you are going to become a God, how in the world are you going to get it? By being out of this world. To what element am I to be, of what function must

147

I maintain, to what thought and to what degree must I focus in order to understand that which I cannot phrase? Don't you understand that everything you know in this life is nothing new and most of that, not one of you contributed to the experience. Sexual intercourse is not new, making children is not new, cohabitation is not new. You didn't invent it, though some of you could swear that you have been the answer. You did not invent it. You have not contributed to your program.

I am a bright and shining star in your program because you made it here to school. That was a contribution, but this is what is alarming: You don't know how to create because you have been taught so tightly and your contribution has only been survival and acceptance. You didn't actually create any of these things. This is something that you should be asking yourself because if you are going to be miracle-makers, you have to fundamentally understand why you have not ever stopped to contemplate how you would make an unknown occur using the tools of known isms.

Now you begin to understand the importance of desiring to unify with a Void that is not bound or measurable by structure because it has no limitations. It is the headwaters of all life. If it were limited even by human perception, then what you would want to realize in this lifetime you would never realize because the option wouldn't be yours. God, however you want to call it, must be formless, it must be no thing, it must be the absence of familiarities, it must have the absence of memory because it is the absence of time.

Those of you who have dreaded the Void because there is nothing in it for you — you don't see the white light, gray light, blue light, or any light, and you sit there and pick your nose and scratch your hindquarters because you are idol worshipers — know this: it is a truth. And as long as you are idol worshipers, you cannot create like a master can create. A master is so naked of expectations in the formula of constructs that the master itself is naked. They don't think in terms of limitation. The platform that you are going to dip into to create, you must accept has no face, no body, no voice. There is no angel talking to you. There is no guide. Stop being a prima donna. Start being humbled to accept knowledge that humbles you to expect greatness. God is "Is." It isn't the star, though it is. It isn't the child, though it is. It is not the morning because it is the night, and it is not the night because it is the morning. It is the enigma of photosynthesis. It is maple syrup and it isn't. It is from where all of those things came.

You have to stop being idol worshipers. You have to stop expecting to see something when you go to the Void. You are so ordained in wanting to see something because unless you see something, you don't believe you are there so you are always questioning and you are missing out. And the army is marching past you, and the saffron dust is in the air and is scattering in your auburn locks and on your black lashes. In order to make known the unknown, there can be no concepts of constructs.

What a knot this is, because look at who you are, look at the garment. You are God's garment but the garment has taken on its own personality and its own agenda. It likes its senses. It is itself because of its senses. That which should be radiating through it has been locked because it is animated of the world and, because it is, it must see animations in the world in order to give validity to itself. The garment has taken on its own personality so what do you suppose, if you are really your garment, you are going to be looking for when you are taking those powerful breaths in C&E®? Are you really taking them or are you just blowing because it is a habit? This school is where you want to be because it is a safe place, but are you really into this? In other words, what is going on in the back of this little memorized motor up here in your head is that you don't feel like blowing because you can't see the energy in your first seal.

Let's have a little awakening here. You have it there in your first seal, and let's show you just how powerful consciousness and energy is. I know many of you who have erections daily and you have them because you think about them. The moment you think about it, the energy in your loins produces an erection. That is a little miracle, that you should be raising your hand on a daily basis. I was a man. I know. So the garment performs a little miracle every single morning. Consciousness and energy is creating the nature of reality. That is real, and it is going to die too. It doesn't look good in the worm's mouth. If consciousness and energy is creating the nature of reality and energy indeed is sitting in the first seal, an erection is its immutable proof because how else do you explain that instantaneous miracle of the human body? It is coming from this brain.

When you are blowing, because you cannot see this energy you really don't believe it is there. The next time you are blowing and you find yourself going unconscious, I want you to remember this little anecdote because that energy is sitting there. It is sitting in the first seal and it is so potent, it can create a human being. That is how powerful it is. It is not filthy; it is powerful. The trick is to get it from the first seal to your brain because if it can create a life-form in the nest, it can create a brain, open and alive. It is the same energy that does this, and the distance is from here in the first seal up to here in your head.

I want to talk to you because I have watched how you let your mind do other things and you start to yawn and move around and are not focused. Remember your erections and remember that it is soft tissue and the flow of blood. Something caused that to happen and that is powerful energy. So the next time you start blowing, I want you to know that a focused breath can move the fire from the loins to the brain, and that is your proof.

How about going to the Void? Where is the Void? The Void is a breath away. The Void is not what you see with closed eyes but rather what you perceive as a conscious thought, and the perception is "nothing," this inky, transparent, midnight blue with faded fragments of borders seemingly to the peripheral vision. You only see those borders because you still think you are seeing with human eyes, so the consciousness is even tunnel blind. Consciousness can see 360 degrees, except you haven't allowed it because in the grid we see with our eyes, not with our consciousness.

Do you know why you don't go to the Void like you think you should? Because you are idol worshipers. You are expecting for something to happen. Don't you understand that in the midst of creation, in the womb of creation, the act of coming to analogical mind in a deep focus of midnight blue is a blessing? There are no distractions; the focused thought can be the only reality you know. If you are expecting to see something, you are primitive. "Nothing" is the blessing.

When you know that and voluntarily desire to experience it, then the engines of the first three definitions begin to roll. The more naked that you can become, the less you care what your name is; it doesn't matter there. You don't care about your social security number. You don't care what you are thinking about, you don't care about your image, you don't care what you look like. You don't care what your body is doing but that it is stable and you are a free agent. The free agent is not a fool. The free agent fulfills number two, to make known the unknown. It must become so unknown to itself that only in dressing in nothing can the miracle happen. You fall to a state, you get into the Void, you power-breath to this place. You pick that raw energy, that is tomorrow morning's erection, and move it to the brain with as much passion as it takes to create an erection, except you are opening your brain with it. And you blow, and in every breath the power comes up.

If you are focused on making that happen, then number one is going to go into effect, consciousness and energy. If you are focused on moving it from down here to your brain, then you already know what you want if the knowingness is there. You have to focus on the knowingness, and with every breath — every long, powerful breath that comes out — it is moving. You do more and it moves, and the focus is steadfast and nothing else exists. The music is becoming dull, and the only thing is this ringing in your ears. If you are that focused on moving it up there, it will happen and your head will explode with energy. That is riding the light, floating, having a head as large as this room. It could be said, in sexual terms, that it is a mental orgasm, that it is the kundalini.

What happens when you float? As you have been stripped of your body — the measurement of your arms, the density of your gut, the height and depth and roundness — the character of your being as that no longer is and can fit into this state of awareness, then you are naked and you want more. And with a focused consciousness you take another powerful breath and you find a hole in the Void. If you think there is one, it will be there, and the hole will be passing through the grid. Once you pass through the grid, you turn around, take one powerful breath, leap up, and fall backwards. And what is it that you see? The midnight sky. You go deeper and deeper and deeper, and you are falling inwards. Falling is symbolic to the subconscious mind of this procedure. That is what it means. And you fall, and go deeper and deeper — this is called blissful focus — and the focus is about falling.

What is it that you are carrying in your being, in yourself? What treasure are you carrying? What are you taking to God? You fall and fall and fall, and the treasure is sweet surrender, to go analogical because going analogical brings the unknown into a known experience. And your first great experience is that perhaps for the first time in your entire schooling here, you actually understood moving energy with focused will. You sat there and focused and made it happen, and riding the light was so blissful that it was now an extraordinary experience.

Surrendering and thinking of nothing, be nothing except surrendering — falling as if you had been dropped from the canopy of midnight and you are falling backwards through space — that is the long-thought focus all the way to no memory. And no memory is closing the gap and bringing it all the way to God. And when you come out of that very slowly, you are going to be a changed human being. You are going to be bearing with you the gifts of your adventure, and the gifts of your adventure have feeble words to explain them. But something is going to transform you like magic and magically you will be transformed. The more you do this, the deeper the transformation, the deeper the initiation. That fulfills number one, number two, utilizing number three.

Draw a key to the side or beneath the three statements:

*Consciousness and energy
creates the nature of reality.*

Make known the unknown.

*The Void,
one vast nothing materially,
yet all things potentially.*

The key is focus — no thinking, a stilled mind — and that is the key. How do you develop focus? Through repetition of initiations daily, every morning. If you focus before you go to sleep, you may not sleep. That is the key. Surrender is what is meant by becoming naked. Flesh and blood can never enter the kingdom of heaven, never can. Consciousness is the only invited guest, and consciousness must come without its garment. You are a garment trying to take on its own luster when in fact you should be the instrument in which a God can radiate through. You are here to learn to be a God radiating through flesh and blood.

The miracles will be small and they will come in groups. Then a larger one will come, and to your ability to accept, they will get larger and larger and will become more common. The more you do this — surrendering under midnight — the more focused you become, the more powerful the reality that you wield.

These are very simple little notes but within them hold the secrets to a seventh-level master, a multidimensional entity, an impressive master who has the magic to make things happen. Deciphering those little statements takes a hierophant, and I am your hierophant.

I want you to have an opportunity to realize the importance of not only this school but the

mighty devotion that you need for it. Whatever you do, do it for the sake of going naked,
making known the unknown, going as deep
and surrendering into nothing as you can. You
must realize here and now that in order to be
miracle-workers, and perhaps one day a light
unto the world, this is how you do it — or you
can work for thirty years.

My beautiful people, do this because you
want this. Have the hunger, find the warrior,
and answer the question, "Why are you here?"

A Great, Timeless Being Worth Remembering

*"Then you can be called the Christos — the
Christ — fully manifested, fully empowered
and endowed, no aging, no dying, a
timeless being with awesome and terrible
abilities. One day I will have turned out
Christs from this school and the world will
rejoice, for this is the mission."*
— *Ramtha*

I want you to know you are beautiful. In
order to be a great being of renown, an entity

159

worth remembering, you have to become humbled, you have to become greater than your senses, you indeed must become formless in the ways of thinking in order to be resurrected into memorable greatness.

The most beautiful entity is one who is on the path of humbling, to surrender to a greater power than its limited means. This is a school where it actually works. It actually is a truth that those crumbs, those little miracles, come from the table of the Lord of Hosts, the creator of everything, and that this most eminent essence is what radiates through you when there are cracks.

You are here because you have what it takes to one day have surrendered in the path to the remarkable journey, to the depths of the subconscious mind. This journey is to have been the lord of the material world, the morning bird's melody, to have loved and adored completely and surrendered from one solitary, small, fearful creature to an eminent richness and excellence of life that knows no boundaries. You are here because you have what it takes. When it is long past your fifth year in this school, you will not have memories of your hurtful past, only the warm glow of irritations that have been covered in pearls.

One day when all your illusions have been disillusionized, when you are greater than your little fears and your little habits — a being that for the most part is difficult for you to imagine except in perhaps that which is termed I, to imagine yourself being so transferred of this moment — that is what it would be like to be a true master of this world. You would be one who does not think but ponders the long, quickening thoughts that are alert, given full attention, and created. It would be one who does not harbor anger or meanspiritedness, does not harbor jealousy or envy, or the childish and petty things of their humanity.

Imagine a being that doesn't think but is. Imagine a being that in spite of the whole world has become so humbled that when you ask it, "What are you?" it says to you with a depth of radiance in its eye, "I am what I am." And "am" is all that is reckoned with in the seen and the unseen.

You may not make it all the way. You may find a comfort zone and stop along the way. The army is going to march, because never has there ever been assembled in the reckoning of humanity a temple so vast as this small one that housed so many humans, mixed humans, men and women in the same confines, in all colors and all ages. Never, ever has there been attempted to bring into one hall so many people so potentially ready to become masters.

Throughout the centuries there have been only fragments of mighty, great entities invisible to the world who have lived thousands upon thousands of years, who every generation changed their name, never die, and live for the sake of preserving the truth. They are the golden threads in the tapestry of humanity of all of its histories, its times. They live because they are the only elements that have preserved a truth that slowly and most certainly has been denied in the human being since the advent of the Gods. The truth that has been so well hidden, so buried, has been that the human being is of the divine essence that any and all Gods ever were, and that so mighty are they that if they possess the truth of a focused ability, not Gods nor nations here, above the Earth, in the Earth, on the Earth, or beyond the galaxy could enslave them because you cannot enslave a consciousness that is fearless.

These magnificent beings that have pre-served the truth — nameless, many names, wearing many disguises — have waited since the dawn of humanity in quiet observance of a hall just like this one and, in fact, is this one. They are watching in awe and steady thought at the possible evolution of so many human beings to a truth that they have lived thousands of years just to preserve so it would not be lost.

Why am I intent upon the sacredness and righteousness of this school? Why is it that I have no compassion or kindness for imitators, the rapers of these words that use them for their own ends, their own glorification and enslave-ment? Because they take the words and wash them through the dirty rags of their grid and give it to a hungry people that only ends up in taking from them yet another trust, another hope, because it will not work.

Like people of all ages wanting the secret, the secret elixir — the hallucinogenic drug, the way in which to open the brain in any way — des-perate to understand themselves but knowing there is a reason to search, there are people who take the teachings and abuse them. They wash them through their dirty grid and the people lose faith again, lose trust again. When they tried this through another means and it didn't work, they will not be back, for they have not seen the miracles that some of you have created and are going to create — a righteous indignation. I defend my own words and they are mine, not spoken in any other school save this one. All of my attention is on you. If you can say that the Ram has focus — oh, I have focus — my focus is large enough to hold the lot of you in it and those of you that have not come yet.

Why have I contracted to a timely being? Why are there entities that have held this truth together for ages? Imagine what you are learning, being the cause for an entity to survive hellfire to preserve it. Why? Because one day given what you possess as a wee little thing inside of you, you have the ability and the potential courage to be a being far different than the one that is sitting before me, a being of immutable power, a luster so rich, so radiant, so loving and powerful. You are not going to go home to where I go. You have to manifest home, as is the duty of one who truly is not a filter unit for the radiant thought, the radiant consciousness that flows through them.

A master is not an editing machine but a vehicle of creative experience fulfilling all three statements. Then you can be called the Christos — the Christ — fully manifested, fully empowered and endowed, no aging, no dying, a timeless being with awesome and terrible abilities. You are going to manifest God for the world through the only thing that the human being never realized existed in the humble human, so just maybe your destiny is greater than you ever thought. Is it possible that in the years to come you could be so deeply initiated that a whole host of you could literally be the new consciousness, the light unto the world brightly shining? God doesn't come in a spaceship, doesn't manifest in a cloud, but God manifests through the human being. That is my intention. That is my modus operandi. One day I will have turned out Christs from this school and the world will rejoice, for this is the mission.

What about all of those silent faces that watch in the shadows? You have all been observed, don't you know? You are the first and only assemblage of this magnitude that ever existed and ever dared to exist. One day this fragile, fragile, beautiful school will produce what has not been produced on this plane in a long, long time.

There are potentials sitting in this audience and that is why you are here instead of the people starving, the people without a home, those with disease. They have every reason to have passion to turn it all around, and if given the opportunity, they would. But there is something that has to occur in an entity that can take the long journey.

You may not make it. You may not make the initiations. You may give up, you may throw it away or stop learning, but I will march past you. If I were here only to deliver to you a philosophy, I would have delivered it long ago in your time already, and it stands on its beauty. They will never figure out if I was really who I said I was or I was just this woman playing an elaborate hoax — what a hoax that would be — but the teachings will always live.

I have an ulterior motive for being here, to fulfill the mandate of recognizing the lowly human being for what it always was — a forgotten God.

This is what I want to add as a final note.

Don't take for granted what you are learning. And if you wanted to learn a piece of wisdom straightaway, then you would begin tomorrow by joyfully taking on and testing for yourself certain apparitions of materialization. Here is a clue: Focus always for three straight days. The focus means that you can focus early in the morning for some time, and the time is up to you. I wouldn't say focus for an hour because that limits the amount that you can create.

Focus every day for a period of that day, and then let your mind come back to it off and on for three days. You cease the focus for three days and then you do it again. At the end of that cycle you should have the runners of your materialization. If you do not, then this is what is going on: Either you don't want it, you don't want to change because of it, or you doubt your focus. It is worthy finding out which of these is at work against you and take the sword out and give the beast a beating.

And then to your delightful amazement, your knowing ability will improve in that six-day stretch. If you name this a routine, all the things you focused on would be so expectedly simple that there would be no argument from the monster about what you are going to do next. You would just do it and it would just be. If I were you, I would do these things.

So be it.

I love you.

PART 3
FUTURE MIND AND THE GARDEN
OF FANTASTIC REALISM

Toast to the Gladiators of the Future

O my beloved God,
I shan't waste away
and linger in the past
one more heartbeat.
I belong to the future.
I declare this day
I am an entity of destiny;
I am an entity of destiny.
I belong to the future.
I shall transcend
these troubled waters
to march to the other side.
This I do proclaim
most earnestly,
in supreme confidence,
that I am this day
what say I.
So be that.
To life and the future.

9. The Ripple Effect in the River of Time

*"Mind is what we call the ripple effect of
reality. We create reality and then the
reality starts to spread out
in the river of time."*
— *Ramtha*

I always know about an entity by what their bands are doing. The future isn't way out there; the future is within your bands. You can always tell where the future is. Some people are body/mind consciousness so their future is brightest around their body. And there are others that mind is their greatest asset so mind starts to dazzle, in that rainbow of your bands, brighter out there versus narrow in here. As mind begins to ignite itself through the consciousness and energy that is surrounding you, as those bands light up I know where your mind is. That means then your mind is going towards the future rather than collapsed in on your body. If everything is about your body and every decision is about your body, then mind isn't in the future; it is in the body. It is body/mind consciousness.

You can see entities where they are in their mind because mind is what we call the ripple effect of reality. We create reality and then the reality starts to spread out in the river of time. When you talk about the wave of reality, the stone that goes into the river and the ripple that goes out from it, the ripple is our mind. You can't talk about reality as if it is somehow disconnected from your mind.

Where do you put mind and reality? They are intricately the same thing. Your reality in people, places things, times, and events — and ideas — is where your mind is. That is the ripple, the frequency specific that begins to encompass all other frequency specifics of other minds that begin to come together in harmony, in union. So mind is reality. A person can have large castles and estates and lands and have whole tribes and people who are their friends, but all of them have small minds. Mind isn't about how large your land is or how small it is. It is something much more vast than that.

You can take this simple master who just tends the ferry boat crossing and likes that particular job because that beautiful work allows him to understand the crossing of the river.

His mind is vast, and it is the gardener effect, planting the seeds of mind so that reality can bloom enormously. Sometimes it takes many years in a lifetime under study to grasp all of these abstractions and plant them. Planting in the ripple effect allows the space for all of this to flourish and come. Some people never realize their work in one lifetime but work their lifetime because we are evermore. That work then begins to bloom in the extended time of the next lifetime. Masters who have learned to master death, their realities continue to move on because their body has changed according to the reality and they are living on to engage them.

Mind is not the concept that a person has a large mind because they have a lot of things or a person who only has very few things doesn't have a large mind. That is ignorant and an injustice. When I look at entities I see where they are. Their mind says everything. What is their mind? Their mind is the fundamental ground design of all the people, places, things, times, and events in their life. You can see an elevation, that where their brightest consciousness is flowing is where the mind is activated and washed out to. And as it is washed out to that, we see that this entity is processing vast consciousness, where they have grown and changed. They are less concerned about those elements of their personality that I have taught you and worked vigorously on. They left those concepts and now are reaching into more abstract ones. They are leaving the tangible and are working into the abstract. They are setting the ground that those abstract thoughts, those I am becoming, those that I have already been, can now grow in. Mind is the ground that causes the quantum field to spring up these ideas into physical reality.

It is also mind that connects every entity on the planet and off the planet. Indeed it is mind that says that we are frequency specific with this person, that person — this and that group, not this or that group — that allows the harmony, the connection. Mind aggregates sameness. When an entity is growing and they are beginning to grow into the abstract, then they are growing into the future because their mind has never been into that level of consciousness. If the mind has never been there, they cannot communicate or indeed be connected to the people who have already possessed that frequency, who already know those ideas, and are already sovereign in a realistic environment. You are just now starting to move frequency towards them. It is the ground of mind that makes that connection, and it is only on that path that these connections are made.

One could see then in throwing the stone into the river that its most dramatic aspect is on impact. But we see the ripple grow and as it grows and expands it reaches other perimeters. Waves in the ocean, any movement in the ocean, causes waves to go on and on and on. Think of that movement as mind, and so the mind is able to touch the shore. The impact was in the center of the river but mind reached the shore. That is visible in you because it is in your bands. If you think of the future as some far remote place, you are mistaken. The future is right here, on the perimeters where your bands are working, where your mind is set up within the consciousness and energy that is holding you together. Whatever part of those bands is activated, where it stops is where the future begins.

When we begin to process and fire new knowledge and then put it together with experience, firing the two together wires them together. That becomes the seed that sits in the ground of mind and begins to grow. That is called destiny. We are planting the future, planting ideas outside the perimeter where our mind is. Our mind then moves to become that ground. And when we wire together, fire together, and wire this completely, then the utilization and the reinforcement of that wiring every day is to keep mind into the future — every day. As we keep mind into the future, we are bringing from that place, that ground, all others who are at the same future. They are frequency specific with you; the ideas are frequency specific with them.

I can assess whether you do the work because I can see it. It is not what is looking in your face; it is what I am looking at when I see you. I can see where you dropped it or took a few steps back and negotiated with your past. I see that we have evolved mind and those who didn't have rolled it up and gone back. That is what we see in the bands, in this pulsating soap bubble around you. It is very elastic. You can see it expand and contract. It is a living thing. It is like the sun coming out in your garden, and all of your little flowers that were asleep at night perk up and go to the light. It is beautiful. They go to the light, and when the light goes away they go back down.

A Mind Frequency Specific with the Future and Its Effects on the Body

"You are growing into a new identity for yourself and you are cultivating it like the garden. You are firing the map, and every day you work to experience that map so that the map and the experience are wired together, this advanced idealism is now producing advanced realism. It is called truth in experience, and in truth in experience we have once again the extraordinary and beautiful play of mind."
— *Ramtha*

Wiring a concept with experience allows you fundamentally to have support of that idea through the experience. But you have to make a choice, whether you stand here or go back to your past. If you go back, you lose this future and are entrenched once again back in your past and so your future has rolled backwards. It doesn't roll forward. However, if you look at this and say, "I must feed this every day, I am the God that must become what I say," the more this hardwiring becomes harder and harder. If we can hold it and let it roll on into the future, other neurons are going to start making connections that expand the idea, and the ground of mind is now producing results. And you know you have a time lapse in neuroplasticity because it can easily slip off and go someplace else if not reinforced. Now our mind has rolled over into a group of like-thinking, like-being people. Every one of them has one element in common with you, and that element is they all agree they are this or that, or they are visionaries of the future, extraordinarily productive, have vision, backbone, and are not victimized by where they are. The victims of the future live in the past, back in that mind, because in the world of commerce, neuroeconomics says this is the most conservative ground to be on. This is safe. "It is difficult but I know it and can be here."

People go, "Oh, yeah, you are right. That was risky. I would never go there. Oh, this is silly. It is all conspiracy. It is bull, it is cow, it is camel, it is fish." And look how many people agree with you. How can so many people be wrong? That is the tribe.

Neuroeconomics, that you are starting to get some definitions on, is your modern term. It isn't my term. Neuroeconomics is talking about real visionaries who really don't have the emotional insecurity of the tribe. It is just turned inside out. In a crowd that is frequency specific, not everyone will agree with you absolutely on everything. There is not a perfect mirror to you of anyone in the future. It is the mind, as it grows, that is the perfect mirror, so all these people agree with you in the future. They all have the same idea. They are frequency specific with you. They are working with you. But then they have other issues. They say, "How could I have been so wrong?"

"Well, you are not."

"But how could you be this way?"

"Well, how could you be that way?"

What we find in the future when we go there is like a child growing up discovering possibilities. And you are frequency specific with the possibilities and things start happening: objects start appearing, visits from extraordinary people start happening. You do that. This is what we agree on. But if you are looking for someone else to agree on something else, that person may be over there, but you only share two points. Everything else is their own view, but they are still in the future.

You have to grow to a maturity as you progress to the future to understand that in people, places, things, times, and events that come from the ground of mind and that you are activated, when you stand in the future this is all your mind. This is all your mind because everyone here is frequency specific with the idea or they have progressed along. They are already doing it, engaging in it. And it could be any one thing that you are discussing. It could be joy, everyone is happy, and you just start drawing a resource of people because they are in the future and have left the past behind. They are their own resource and perhaps that is your connection. Everyone is well, of vibrant health, that are all ages, and that is your connection. That is what you have. They are all your mind.

When we go back, we have people breaking down and perhaps that is the connection. In the future then, you may have found genius because that is what you are working on. Genius: You can't define it other than the simplicity of seeing the extraordinary in common things, the advancement and the betterment of something. Now we are in an area where all these people are geniuses and you are now frequency specific with them. You can sit down and talk into the wee hours. You can take rides on incredible flying machines because that is your mind. They are your mind. They may be in the future and you are connected. You have come this far in personal growth and just completely shifted neighborhoods. You are growing into a new identity for yourself and you are cultivating it like the garden. You are firing the map, and every day you work to experience that map so that the map and the experience are wired together, this advanced idealism is now producing advanced realism. It is called truth in experience, and in truth in experience we have once again the extraordinary and beautiful play of mind.

We begin to run into people, go unexpectedly to places, have unexpected things, share unexpected times, and engage those through events that we could never have fathomed before. You would be frequency specific with all of that, indeed you would have harmony with it and, moreover, you would be experiencing it.

The new self that is being cultivated here

begins to advance itself as mind and begins to produce truth. It says, "This is who I am. This is what I have done."

The child's vision when it is born is downloaded already — you were downloaded, everyone was downloaded — with the map of the soul that says this is what you haven't learned, this is what you need to complete, these are the gifts of genetics you will have in modeling this map. Your gene pool will quirk out a few gifts, and you are blessed with these gifts, those opportunities, so everyone has a fair chance. But you are in a body specific. It has been specifically designed to have the mind that meets the challenges indeed, that turns emotion into wisdom so that we have completed that part of the divine created in us making the journey. We work to do that, learning perhaps the greatest advice spiritually is that your greatest emotional challenge is your greatest work because that is just unfinished business. It is unfinished in making a reality and breathing into it the breath of life so that now it can be given up and you are free to continue the work and continue on.

Everyone has the perfect body, the perfect vessel. You already do. If you subscribe to the concept that you are immortal, you must overcome all your emotions because they are intricate in you. You must own them. Your DNA will respond and you will absolutely be functioning in creating yourself an evolved body. Your body will begin to change. Its frequency cannot be in opposition to the leadership of what you have made a decision on. The List, the Neighborhood Walk®, if absolutely and supremely executed in presence and confidence, spreads the mind. It also changes the body in evolution. The body gets changed if the mind is changed. There is a sequence: The body gets changed, the mind is manifesting the reality, and the body is capable of experiencing the jubilance of new opportunities. Bodies don't die as long as you are evolving.

10. How Do We Grow New Neurons into the Future and the Unknown?

"Your brain is already downloaded with the mind of God, dependent upon levels of consciousness that it functions through. It is as complex as all of the stars that shine, all of the galaxies, all of the universes that hang in the Void. It has all that information. The brain is the greatest supercomputer ever built because it was built by God."

— Ramtha

Your journey was to learn many, many spiritual concepts to garner the best of civilization's science to help support these concepts that can so easily be forgotten or washed into the dregs of religion — good and bad, right and wrong, and punishment — and all of that rules the day. We can lift our Spirit out of new ideas, the radical idea of inwardly changing ourselves, that now you have the science to actually fundamentally do that. It was always there but you needed someone bigger than me, better than me, to tell you that what you think, you create, which is now coming to the surface in science everywhere.

You can rely on that now. It is not arbitrary any longer. It is not whether you like me one week and don't like me the next and throw out everything I have said and keep a few things, you know. It is not arbitrary. You reached a level that scientifically says you have the capacity to cure alcoholism, depression. You have the ability to heal yourself, to grow younger, to reverse in yourself catastrophic damages. You have the ability to grow brand-new neurons with a new thought simply by walking. You don't have to run; all you have to do is walk.

Neurogenesis takes place in a walk in focused thought. When you are doing something, you are having a thought and you are firing them together. Now we are getting new concepts. That is what makes the brain young. You know through science that you have in you the capacity to generate new neural activity. Could you generate the next step — that science hasn't yet confirmed but will — when I say to you that the mind of God is already downloaded in your brain? You already have neurons that don't have any other history than being joyful. History simply means they were created to have this information. These neurons don't have any other history than the capacity of saying these words to come together and download information from that knowledge. We have proven to you that you have a midbrain that is psychic. Look at the walls in the Great Hall with your remote-views, in case you forgot.

We have proven to you that you have the ability to know the future just through remote-view. Now you have the refreshing confidence that this is innate in you. It was always innate in you. If you have the ability to see the future, you have the ability to know information ahead of time. Where did that information come from? If it hasn't even been broadcast yet — no one has put it on television, it hasn't been seen anywhere but you saw it before it ever was — where did that information come from? It came from your midbrain. That is our evidence that your brain is already downloaded with the mind of God, dependent upon levels of consciousness that it functions through. It is as complex as all of the stars that shine, all of the galaxies, all of the universes that hang in the Void. It has all that information. The brain is the greatest supercomputer ever built because it was built by God. The mind of God is already in here.

How do we work neurogenesis into the activation of new, baby, infantile neurons? Where are they springing from? From a call button turned on in the brain of knowledge. It is turned on in a walk: "I have always been happy. I have always been well, always, always." Where in our brain do we find the neurological activity that will respond to "always," the neurons that have been programmed for you to always be healthy? That is their only history. If we weave them in together with joy, and you weave genius in, and you weave whatever else you want in constructing the new identity, they all fire and start to fire together. They become a collective, a neural group in someone's brain that your history is that you and this group have the information relative, at hand, for this individual and their journey to be happy. This collective has all of the information from the future that is relative to happiness here and it is about joy and genius. This collective already has that. That is your history. You don't have other collectives' history; you have your history.

Let me get you to turn around and hold hands; reach across and touch each other. Imagine you are a neuron. So what we have here in this group is a history of joy and we have the history of genius relative to you in this other group. They are all firing together.

We are going to ask them to be really acrobatic for a moment. I want genius to let go of joy for a moment and hold hands with this other group, which is health. We are going to have the collective of genius and health holding hands. Joy, you come on in too. Now we are really happy and we are feeling good. Now over here to this group, "I have always been fabulously wealthy," you are the wealthy group. Your history is only wealth.

You are doing excellently. Let's see. "For as long as I can remember" — don't unlatch; we just wired you together — you have to go home together now. What we have done is declared ourselves filled with joy. We have downloaded the future, future genius, and we are happy about that. We have glitter going.

We then said, "I have always been radiantly healthy." The history of health got in on this picture, and last but not least you have a little cash to boot. This sort of looks like a Gordian knot. We want them to stay intact, so we are saying this all day long. We have to utilize our opinions through joy. It is not good and bad; we are still filled with joy. We have to utilize not that we don't know — I am stupid, I am dumb, I am insecure, I am incapable. We will never go there again. We only utilize "I have always been a genius and I do download the future." That is our position. That is clear. And they are firing "I have always been healthy."

You could start out this journey by not seeing too well and not having a lot of energy. It would be contraire if you want to say how you want to feel. You just go, "I am this," and that just keeps it going. Even if we were feeling that way, we have to come over and go, "For as long as I remember, I am radiantly — let me put on my glasses to read this — I am radiantly healthy." Radiant health, fire over here your history, and somehow you get a little glitter going in you. Immediately when that fires its history, it releases adrenaline.

All of a sudden these people start walking a little better because it is changing, and of course their DNA is manufacturing this code. This group tells DNA which codes to make those essential proteins and the energy level of the cell itself. If the energy is coming from the cell, if they are the group that will have their way in their future, the energy level in the cell has just jumped a hundred percent — a hundred percent.

This is the new map, the new self, and we have their history. Their history then works within its group. And as we begin to start experiencing people, places, things, times, and events, we start feeling better and other opportunities come our way. In the collective group of opportunities, all these opportunities have a history, a new frequency association. When we have to have a bridge to our wealth, it is going to require a deeper level of what we want to do about it. Those are new neurons that just activated, and we are talking about our joy. These are new opportunities that came into our picture that activated the history of other neurons that are deeper, waiting on the periphery to assist in making the pictures of reality that caused the mind to ripple. There are opportunities, research, science, that have come in to benefit. There are opportunities that are wealth, the future, joy. Now that the picture was fired by the individual core, reality is starting to happen, experiences are starting to be experienced, bringing with them a plethora of reality of new people, places, things, times, and events. This is new history opportunity that comes in to the initial core. It is a maturation, indeed a maturing of who we say we are. It starts to come, our knowledge begins to increase, our activity begins to increase, and relatively so does mind and reality.

In this collective group we have alien cultures and people from the future, a lot of people from the future. Those that are coming to the periphery are people coming from the future because now you are encroaching on it, firing associative memory — coming in, experience, new neurons, new realities — and mind is growing. Now we are into the future. But what is the future? We have made it past a difficult time. We are on the other side. We placed our frequency there. We started the work, so we have alien cultures here and the neurons needed to communicate with alien technology. We are frequency specific and have grown to that level. We have added to that level its history, and here they are. Furthermore, we are in the future of times of people you can't see. We have grown to that area, and when we hit alien technology, we do a time shift. As we grow, we start moving from this picture of time to another picture of time to another picture of time because we have left this time.

As we begin to make time shifts that will begin to occur in 2009, 2010, and 2012, if I can encourage you to begin to work on time shifting from that point on, we have actually moved out of one parallel universe and we are starting to move into another. This, what you are part of, is how students of the Great Work began to train. They began to train by having the courage to change, to leave the tribe, leave their father's house, and begin the arduous journey of replacing perception with creation. That started in the core group. Every experience that was added was an evolution that evolved the student further and further. And be mindful that all of this is already in your head.

Regenesis and Evolution by Your Own Hand

"To assess what is not being used, the multiplicity of choices and options that can come together and be encoded to allow a singular species to meet neuroeconomics by its choice — its spiritual choice, its neural choice — dictates its physical adaptation. Indeed that is called evolution. It is called the caterpillar and the butterfly."
— Ramtha

In neurogenesis, the concept of new neurons growing, they are growing from history. They are the bridge. There is an area called bridge consciousness in our bands and they grow from there. What they do, their utility, and the reason they are important is this. When you began to move neighborhoods — and I affectionately appreciate that this process was named not some medical term but a new neighborhood — it is a move, a change. I most appreciate the simplicity of that. If we look at the beginning work of a neighborhood, it

glistens brightly in the beginning but it is
fraught with the tribe. It is fraught with the old
neighborhood. It is fraught with the thinking
that before — they just came in and you never
looked at them — they just did their work,
checked in, posted their neurological opinion,
and began to cancel out the opportunity.

It is not until we take a look at them that
we begin to realize that this group is firing. Its
armament is fear and doubt and argumentative,
and they slide in. They fire in to depose what
the viewer is being shown, what your God is
being shown. It is not until you begin to look at
just how much you have undermined or have
allowed the undermining of historical neurons
that are hardwired now — they are hardwired.
The only thing that is going to get rid of them
is Alzheimer's or a head injury or a few drastic
acts like that. They are hardwired, and not until
they get calcified will they start to break away.
They are in it. They are in there. This is the
group that is undermining the future possibility.

It isn't until you take a look at it that you
understand that what fires together wires
together, that hope and despair can be wired
together depending upon what you did with it.

And you know your examples: What feels good is painful; that is sadistic wiring. That could be wired in the lack of self-appreciation. So it is a self-punishment that makes you feel good that you are punishing your body for some abstract act, and that is how distorted the neuronet can become through childhood and puberty and postpuberty into the young adult. It can become that hardwired.

The art of understanding that it is and how it got that way is an integral part of an advanced student's journey into the greatness of the future. In this study we also have the power of observation to actually observe one of these networks firing and understand they are just a network. But we also understand how they link into the body, cause it to respond, and drain it of its energy, its vitality — it is getting drained just for an emotional response — and how automatic and unconscious this has been.

We have proven the power of the Observer by the remote-views on the wall, what you yourself have created in the field, your journey in the field and your card, your journey in the labyrinth against all obstacles, how far you went and never gave up. Don't ever forget

those extraordinary gladiator moments in this
school because they stand as a testament that
there is a deity in you watching, watching the
will morph into the extraordinary. That proof
counters doubt and fear and lethargy but if left
unattended, these neuronets undermine it all
because that is their program.

That program of course leads us to the past,
not the future. In this place that we had a line
of demarcation from the past walking onto the
future, the consensus is these are the victims of
a worldwide plan. They are easily manipulated.
How do they prevent knowledge like this from
getting out? By simply saying knowledge like
this is conspiratorial. It is the same spin some
gave when they talked about terrorism and got
you to believe all of that and everything else
they have told you. It is now a lie, always has
been. They can spin you. This group can easily
be spun, just work off the tribe, fear, do everything they want you to do to give you a false
sense of security, and they have had their way
with you. If you hear someone in the future say,
"But I heard that the government did this and
this," and they say back to you, "Well, that is just
outrageous, that is conspiracy theorists," they

will shame you, along with everyone else, back into living here, or saying you are going to die.

The thought processes of hardwiring live in that group. This is where fear comes from. You all have integrated it because that is what protects the boundaries that prevent change. It prevents what we did here in school. Furthermore, it makes you doubt. Of course you should doubt. When did you do anything extraordinary? When did you consider yourself brave? When did you consider yourself highly responsible by taking on your own personal issues? When did you consider yourself personally responsible by tangling with your own grievances, your past, your afflictions, your suffering, your prejudice, biases, and judgments? When were you responsible to rid yourself of pain and suffering that you haven't even realized you got addicted to it? When are you going to do that? When was the last time you were brave? See, that is the group, the group mentality. The group mentality doesn't dare go here. It is entertained, like the Romans did in ancient Rome and gave them the circuses and the games and kept the people wagering on who would win and who would kill this person, how many animals would be slaughtered, and who would be murdered there. You just do it in a more modernized version and your slaughter is to destroy a person's reputation. That is equal to burning them on a cross in the middle of an arena. Everyone does that because that is the safe place. You see, that is what keeps this hardwired.

The consequences of hardwiring keep you in this group because of the lack of spiritual responsibility, the lack of taking a position that maybe you have had experiences — that you have had out-of-body, precognitive, and psychic experiences — and make you question the notation of reality as it is popularly seen. Perhaps you do embrace the concept that you have lived before and will live again. If you do, there is a whole reason, and the next step would be why.

Personal responsibility starts to uncover your neglect in being a virtuous, noble, upright being who really takes on your addictions, and when? When we begin to feel victorious to ourself is when we are no longer insecure. People can say, "Well, you are a conspiracy theorist," and all you do is smile because you are not cowed back into the tribe. You have the courage of personal conviction, indeed the courage of personally working in healing your-self, that real conviction isn't out there; it is in you. It doesn't matter what anyone else says. You don't want their reality; you want your reality. And if you are such a social butterfly, you will never have your own reality. You will be slaves. You already are. You just don't even know it. That is you. And you will not see a new era because it takes personal conviction to change yourself. It takes personal conviction to wrestle with your necromancers, to get unad-dicted from being a victim.

Take responsibility. If I accept that I have lived again, then I am here in destiny to have experienced these incidents that affected me in my life. They are frequency specific to me. No matter how urbane or wretched, there is a link, inarguably. Stand up for the link and take yourself off of the cross; I did. You take yourself off of your suffering cross and be strong enough for a conviction that links you psychically, links you frequency specific to some greater work that leads not only to forgiveness but to the understanding. Forgiveness comes once we are virtuous. Then we understand why people do what they do. But until we become virtuous and wise, we never do. As long as we are caught in the throbbing heart of suffering and pain, we will always be on the victim side because that is what we are. How does that enlighten the world and benefit you? It doesn't.

When you stand for, and you begin, the personal conviction supremely confident that you are going to conquer yourself, you are going to detach all the people you blamed and let them go. You are going to stop eating yourself into oblivion and start being a doer. You are going to start being proactive into sending to your body the most quintessential message that your body will think the gates of heaven have come to relieve it. To assert immortality one has to take that thread and begin to apply it. If I have lived before, there is cause and effect of me living again. I must take this responsibility and start releasing people. You really do. It is extraordinary. It is the Gordian knot. We can do it by sword, we can do it knot by knot, and we change. And if we despair because we cannot find our way in this montage of faceless people and we still want to be different and unique, what is it in you that wants that? It is because you don't have it for yourself.

When you become your own vicar, indeed when you say, "This is why I am the way I am and was the way I am and gives me solid ground and momentum — I have the mental tools to literally release myself from this suffering and begin the conquest" — then you live what you believe in. You live that you are immortal, that you have returned to cause and effect. You are living the act of neutralization to be wise. Now you are genuine, upright, and visible. There are no places in you that are weak. If there are, you take them on. You know how to do that. Add it to the Neighborhood Walk®, to the List, to what you blow out in the power breath. You counter that day with strength and fortitude, that at the end of the day you sleep sweetly, your body is at rest, and your Spirit is flying and not in purgatory.

That hardwiring is what we are after here. It is only neurons with history connected to the body. That is all it is. Nevertheless, we have all of this future potential waiting. In the neurogenesis of new neural activity, there are bridge neurons. They will allow you to get great knowledge and information and keep you from arguing for your limitations. In fact, the army turns in on the limitations and makes war on them because we are now seeing what the program has always been doing. We have the power of observation to change it.

It is the eye of God looking on it that makes this happen. If the intent of the eye of God is to see that you are wretched, limited — whichever one of those hardwired thoughts come in — if the eye of God takes a look at it and knows the intent, God gets rid of it. And you will know, because you didn't know that all the time you were walking around with a weight on your shoulders. You didn't realize how heavy you were. You didn't realize, because you have adjusted emotionally to this, that there was a loss of cellular energy in your body. In fact, you had to get up and go run, work out, play, and do all this stuff to generate an increased heart rate with muscular activity to get a sense of energy for a while which, in a common place, should have been at peak performance going every day, every moment. You didn't even have to walk across the room; you already got it. It is called jazz and is already there. You didn't realize that you were walking around heavy-laden. You didn't know that until the eye of God in the God-scope got to look at one of those thoughts. That broke it and the Neighborhood Walk® broke it.

Suddenly you felt lighter, for you didn't realize you were heavy. Suddenly there is an incredible lightness of being. It may have happened only a few steps while you were here at school. It may have happened in a few moments or may have lasted the whole time. But that incredible presence of lightness is because the burden of body/mind consciousness has been moved. Seemingly an invisible voice and invisible presence of some door that opened which allowed you to go in for the first time — however you want to explain it — simply meant that the burden was lifted. In doing this walk, one felt lighter because we put God onto it with the clear, willful intent that we don't want this burden anymore.

Even if it was for a little bit, that instantaneous, cellular, energetic reward is a light peeking through the door that is opening. Don't close it. Continue to open it up and indeed the metabolism of your cells will only respond more and more to the door opening and the past gone. These genesis and regenesis cells — nerve cells, neurons — are the bridge that grow to help you in that one moment to bind to an experience. That is what they do; they bind. "I have always downloaded the future," and here they come; they bind to it. They in turn truncate to the history of those undermining neurons that will begin to respond. Why are they malleable? Because they will stay with this experience until you replace them with those opinions, and they move right off. This is called plasticity — mobility, plasticity.

The bridge neurons are there and they are mobile. They are not hardwired. They are giving you an opportunity to change the picture. And as you can see, we began to increase the picture of mind in the collective groups we created here, and it was easy to imagine for those of you who were curious. We started with the nucleus, and the nucleus was the stone you threw into the river. And as we did the List, the waves started going out and out and out. All the while those young neurons started in the nucleus when the stone was thrown. They were the bridge consciousness to each collective group that was added, and they were there to either detach or add to the group.

After forty days of continuously living as the breath of God in this experience, the core knowledge came together, the history, the real history. Then we hardwired the group. This is how a student of the Great Work processes thought. It is through this history, this neurological, absolute history.

Imagine for a moment this collective group of genius without beginning to connect. Are they just sitting there being unused history of genius? They are just sitting there being history of unused genius, still getting information from God, but no one is home.

It takes at once courage to be self-responsible and understand that the spiritual work is much more than a bunch of angels flapping silly wings around and sprinkling stardust, having purple-light experiences and crystal mornings and vegetarian nights. Spiritualism is the real work of the Spirit. It is more than past-life experience readings, wishing and wanting, making things that bong and bing, sitting in meditation, and going out there looking like you did and resenting it. That is called a paint job. That doesn't make you great and is not the core of the Great Work.

The core of the Great Work doesn't care what you wear. Furthermore, it doesn't care what you look like. It is not the interest of that globe of energy that is now sitting in the brain. It is called the body electric, electrifying the central nervous system so you can wear this body. It is the same ball of light that goes into the seed of a rose and gives it its dream so it can grow. The same ball of light can do amazing things that is now in here in your head, and it is making this body and it can show you all seven of its bodies. Just because you wear purple doesn't mean that you are a seventh-level entity. Just because you wore crystals around your neck, did that give you clearer spiritual sight? No. This is the Great Work, because Spirit is that which is not seen and that which is not seen is the influence behind the throne, sitting right in your head. It is you and I. We are not seen, but you see us when we appear like this in this frequency. You don't see us like this ball of light because you don't want to see us like this, but that is what we are.

The spiritual work is to begin to decipher all the knowledge that you have learned in this school and linger long years on some knowledge. It is to bring about personal identity and really begin to separate the self of the program versus the one called the God who has come again who lives inside you. The long mechanistic work in this journey is beginning to understand how you programmed this machine but it is not boring or tedious. It is thrilling, on the edge of possibilities, when the philosophy is matched with experience — to see a common person become uncommon, a regular person see Spirit at work — and that has always worked in this school.

We will call it that for a while until we begin to define it under the concepts of the Observer, quantum physics, and the band of reality that leads to all time existing simultaneously. Learning incrementally all the way through the processes is the spiritual journey of ourself. It is understanding how our body works and functions, not as an enemy or an asset but understand its DNA, the seed of its garden, how it was programmed, and understand why. To assess what is not being used, the multiplicity of choices and options that can come together and be encoded to allow a singular species to meet neuroeconomics by its choice — its spiritual choice, its neural choice — dictates its physical adaptation. Indeed that is called evolution. It is called the caterpillar and the butterfly.

11. The Dream of Flight and the Butterfly

"It just dreamed of flight, and the same DNA that made it a caterpillar, that it was originally born with, allowed it to dream. And the dream without time, distance, and space allowed the body to dissolve the past and reconfigure an aerodynamic creature. Beautiful."
— Ramtha

When the caterpillar gives up the past — languishing for the days of heaps of green leaves, is full and content — it makes its own bed and dreams the dream of flight and oriental wings. It is a complete overhaul of what one aerodynamically would need to position itself through gentle breezes and great winds. What would it need to look like aerodynamically? And what would it need to ingest in the form of photosynthesis of sugars? What would be its new fuel? Its fuel would change from the cater-

209

pillar to a butterfly. From eating heavy foliage and breaking it down to sugars, it would drink nectar, the golden elixir of the Gods, because aerodynamically it can process those sugars without bulk. And so it just dreamed of flight, and the same DNA that made it a caterpillar, that it was originally born with, allowed it to dream. And the dream without time, distance, and space allowed the body to dissolve the past and reconfigure an aerodynamic creature. Beautiful.

That is so common in nature and you never see it. If you have met a butterfly, you haven't contemplated it as a messenger. What did this beautiful creature do? That is all you need to wonder and find out and then apply it to yourself. The caterpillar moved to a new neighborhood. The caterpillar in the dream had to call on this entire group that would be linked in every fashion, just labeled a wee bit different. The history of what it was dreaming — all the neurons that brought the dream to pass, its function, its future, its opportunity — all had to come into play with all of its history to provide the dream. That dream unfettered by regret, indeed unpunished, untortured, was free — the dream was free — and allowed complete metamorphosis.

If the God of the caterpillar/butterfly is not the most superb God, I don't know one. You can talk about your Gods of ancient history, your religious deities, but I have not seen one caterpillar turn into a butterfly from them. The God of this metamorphosis is a great God indeed because it is the open book of nature. What God has done here in this miracle of nature is the same God that is in you. It is the same God's history that is in you and is historically downloaded, for it is called the kingdom of heaven. So certainly not everyone wants to be a butterfly but everyone wants to be its equivalent from being a caterpillar. They want to be the equivalent of metamorphosis.

Metamorphosis starts at that demarcation line in your life, moving forward or backwards, whatever you think you are. If you are moving forward and you don't have the operational hookup yet, it will come. It will hook itself up. You just have to stay hooked for forty days and live as a butterfly, think as a butterfly, reason as a butterfly. You cannot argue that once you were a caterpillar. You can't do any of that. You are only a butterfly. That is the new life, and all of the hookups will come into place. It is the most glorious opportunity that you haven't even met yet. You still have to be supremely responsible for yourself, and you continue that journey. You are still on that journey.

The Gardener of Your Own Mind

"The same is true that you belong to the future when you begin to change. The reality, the mind, the ripple effect, as it were, ripples forward to make this space for all of this to become reality within. The ground of mind is the space where that reality took bloom."
— Ramtha

The soil these beautiful flowers are in is the mind. It comes from the Void as well and is filling the space of the Void. This soil is mind. All of the elements that make it up and make it fertile ground we could simply say, in analogy, are wisdom and experiences. What has already been accomplished is what gives us this ground. The fertility of the soil is based upon the decay of old experiences. I love nature. We can explain anything by looking at nature.

In our soil there were three ideas: I have always been filled with joy; I have always been radiantly healthy; I am fabulously wealthy. Healthy, wealthy, joy — I am whatever; it depends upon how many thoughts get fired. We began to concentrate and redefine what we wanted to be, and once we decided, each one of those groupings of joy and genius — consider as a seed, a bulb — got put into the soil, and on and on and on.

In order to nourish this seed, we have to give it the essential elements of life. We must give it water and certain frequency. These flowers are frequency specific with early spring so they are the beginning flora of the Great Work. They won't come back in summer or fall. There are other dreams that are coming in summer and fall. These flowers are all beginnings. In order for them to grow, we have to nourish them with life-giving water to moisten and allow the ground to be permeable so the bulb itself can drink and in its processes of cellular division begin its energetic work, just like you. We have to give it a modicum of light. These early spring flowers require a soft light, not harsh or hard, and a certain frequency.

In other words, they are the beginning of change so they are most gentle and fragile, very fragile. In the beginning then, with water and soft light and the right temperature, all becomes exactly how the new neighborhood begins. Every day, all day long, we rise in the morning, water the soil, and that is simply proclaiming what we are. That is the water of life. Throughout the day as we are becoming it, that the light is shinning on this garden means that God is looking at it all day long. Regardless of what happens, "I have always been happy, I have always been healthy, I have always been fabulously wealthy. It is my frequency." That is the light shining on it, a perfect analogy of God looking through the God-scope at this. The nourishment from nature comes through the quintessential creator of what is important.

What is important is creating the picture and letting God look at it. All of those are nour-ishment, water, light, growth. As it begins to grow, it is growing off of its own internalized energy morphed from photosynthesis. There is where the Observer comes in, where all day long we are going to tend to these little ideas that we have planted in the soil of our mind. As they begin to grow and begin to get strong and peek above the surface, we rejoice because our first runners are coming, our first opportunity. And how can we possibly explain that out of dirt something green came? Where was the color green in there? It came from itself, for it has the ability to grow, and we rejoice. We are starting to see now that an abstract list that we are wiring together is starting to produce experience. It is starting to happen, and the more it happens, the more water comes, the more focus comes, the more jubilance comes, and this stem starts to grow.

When it becomes the optimum experience and blooms is when this idea of joy got consummated. In two weeks' time, three weeks', four days' time, it started to permeate everything. The permeation of becoming what you say, the hardwiring, is the perfume of the flower. And this aromatic perfume is the glitter and the sheer joy of being joy, indeed the sheer smell of success, the smell of a thought into matter that has become. It is the experience of feeling great when you wake up in the morning because you have fueled your cells consistently over a period of time. They now are getting the code and creating energy on a cellular level that to the whole is energetic photosynthesis. You wake up and you are well. Your diseases are going into remission and you are gaining strength. You don't have to do anything; it is coming from within you. And pretty soon in spring our flowers of new thought bloom and fill the ambiance of any theater with the beauty of its smell, and so is the frequency specific of such a gardener. When this has bloomed — it will have already started — other aspects of the garden will start to go. And here they are coming on — the more of who we are and say we are — and the same happens. And what we brought into our garden will have done its work and hardwired you. It will wilt, and all the energy will be pulled back into its seed. It will go into dormancy and wait again until the next spring.

When we put all of this in a pot, we only imagined that we wanted these blossoms. Did you ever stop to think about the destiny of an action, indeed the destiny of this bulb? You say, "If I do everything right, it is going to come out of the ground and give us a beautiful flower and it will smell fragrant." That is true, but you don't go any deeper than that. This flower occupies this space but when it was in the ground, there was nothing in that space. It grew its mind into this space and filled it entirely. You have beautiful bushes, trees, shrubbery, and lovely flora. If you are a wise person you will have planted them. If you go home to your hovels today, imagine your roses pruned back, your trees where they stand. Take a look at how magical their dream is where you can see now your bush will occupy that entire space. It is its destiny. The same is true that you belong to the future when you begin to change. The reality, the mind, the ripple effect, as it were, ripples forward to make this space for all of this to become reality within. The ground of mind is the space where that reality took bloom.

You say, "I have always been filled with the love of God" and "I have always downloaded the future. I have always had that ability. This day I download the future." When you are present — and the sun is looking at what you are saying — and you have kept at bay all that is contraire to what you are saying, letting God look at this, then you are present. And indeed when you are present and you say that, you are causing the ground of mind to ripple to a future which is magnanimous. The ripple is creating a future, and if it is here it can be measured in unlimited miles in time, distance, and space, but it is right to here. Before you lies the fertile soil of the blooming of what you have said, and it begins the day you put it in the pot, the day you say it.

You must be the excellent gardener who nourishes it in the simple requirements of letting God see it, saying who you are, letting the sun shine upon it, and living it. Now it flourishes and in the same space is a humble flower that is relative to the greatness of a God like you. The space of what you say you are will be reserved for your manifestations — that is how magnanimous it is — because all you have to do is take a pot, put those seeds, those bulbs in, cover it up, and say, "Where is the flower? It is yet to bloom. Where is it going to bloom? It is going to come out of the pot. That will be its destiny."

It will bloom up there. Same is for you, butterfly.

12. The New Wave of Reality, the Next Time Shift, Must Come from You

*"Joy is a state of being. You have enough
time to begin to realize inner joy because
you are doing the work. You have enough
time to download the future. You do. You
have enough time to begin the work."*
— *Ramtha*

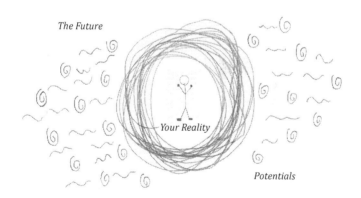

It really isn't so important that I draw because all I would have drawn would be to tell you that this is you, here are your bands, and all this is the future. Then I would have simply said the things that you want are these potentials over here but you are only accessing your reality within these bands that are frequency specific to you. And look at you floating in an endless sea of potentiality — an endless sea — that the moment that you shift, then these bands create the mind out here and these opportunities spring forward and now your reality is growing. Now you are moving to the future and beyond. That is what it looks like. What is the difference between this and the pot? They are the same thing, aren't they? Most people want the wave of reality to happen to them but it must come from you.

Last, I want to say this to you. I cannot make you get up and do this. Lethargy is the disease and destruction of the Spirit. Lethargy falls under the category of lots of excuses: This isn't exciting enough, it is not thrilling enough, you don't believe in it, it is not going to work, you doubt it. All those excuses live in the category of neurons that are hardwired.

It is like Michelangelo's painting of "The Creation of Adam" where God reaches out and we are just a little too tired to straighten our finger out. All we would have to do to straighten it out is to see it straight. I cannot cure that in you. I can do things to you. I can endeavor to get you to analyze something, bring you down and put you in a place that you have to contemplate like I did in my life. Just take a look at it and see what you really are from an angle of nature.

You can belong to either group. The destiny of the world is set by those who own it. I said to you many years ago in your time, you cannot take that number, that chip that is going to be implanted in you. You cannot do that. At that point you will be soulless. Those are words far from the past going forward to show you the reality of it. You just can't do it.

You can say, "But I want to." Then please do. But individual will and sovereignty will really get locked down. It will be harder to dream the dream, to do the work when you are owned, and you are already owned to a lot of degrees. Now is the time not to be lazy. Now is the time to begin the processes of new neurological change, that the neurological change still has time knowing how slow you are, how fraught with excuses you have become — just knowing you.

Many of you have already advanced from joy to the future, to health, made those changes, and started to see the bumps coming up out of the soil. The excitement of actually watching that is in itself its own energy, and all the cells are behind it. It is producing its own energy machine. Once you begin to see the results of just how remarkable you are, then it starts to spread. You have enough time, within a certain time, to get with it because at a certain time you will have already been so wired and so knowing how to do this that you could be wiring the next level of technology for yourself and the next time shift.

The difference between you and masters who are conquering themselves is that they have inward self-respect, take responsibility, and make changes. That leads to inward joy, inner joy. It would be of little effort to set them on a journey to eclipse time because they would come to the understanding that all is energy with information. Not one is greater or lesser than the other. These entities can go forward in time and bypass everything and live in a different reality than the one that is coming down here because they are wired to do that.

When will you do that and start it in this nucleus and start to go forward? You have a lot of time to become more prosperous than your fair share. You have much time now to counter twenty, thirty, fifty, sixty — whatever the number is — years of rotten living to turn it around in your body and let your body sing with energy. You have enough time to do that. You have enough time to get happy. Joy is a state of being. You have enough time to begin to realize inner joy because you are doing the work. You have enough time to download the future. You do. You have enough time to begin the work. But it sounds so hard, doesn't it, forty days?

What did you do the last forty days? "Well, I traveled, I cried a lot, talked to people, went out to dinner." Are any of those assets going to take you forward? So what did you do the last forty days? Why couldn't you have just done this wiring for forty days knowing, hardwiring a concept and then allow the opportunities to bloom in front of you instead of hunting for them?

You still have time. You cannot have a mind that is functioning in a very bright frequency and have it enslaved by something as mindless as the graymen who have stupefied everyone. These two don't mix.

Frequency specific brilliance is not going to be caught in the net of stupidity. It just won't.

In the interim, nature will be your hero, catastrophically speaking, in many ways. The graymen have contributed to it all and are even trying to control it. None of that works. By 2010 your icecaps will have melted. Where are you living? How close to the water are you living? Can you be a foster parent to a polar bear? Nature is going to rid this and in such prophetic visions seen for eons of this time — of this time — because it has to. If you continue to consume your resources, if you refuse to be a genius in energy transportation, then you are letting wars go on. Do you know how many people have died for your tank of gas? You don't want to think about it, but why shouldn't you? Do you know how many people have perished because they had to give up their plantations so that you could enjoy your fruit? Do you know how many people? You call it worldwide organization.

As long as there is another hole to drill to sap the energy out of the Earth, they will not allow a new technology, even though it is coming. But who is going to want which one? Sometimes you have to take what the people are spinning to you to go against. It is called radical behavior, radical thinking. They tell you that there isn't enough sunlight, there isn't enough technology for hydrogen fuel cells, there isn't this and that, and the only solution is oil. My God, that is because they own it all. They have done away with so many people just to fill that SUV up and keep it going because you are going to want it, but you haven't done anything. Now that has consequences. Nuclear fuel should be fought against in all corners. You can't talk about the logic with these people who throw barrels of nuclear waste down through fault lines and volcanoes, thinking that somehow the furnaces of the Earth will purify it. It does not work that way.

The energy is free all around you. There is an automachine that has come out of France that simply runs on compressed air and you just fill it up with an air pump. So where do you get the power to run an air pump? From the sun. How hard is that? "But it won't look good." So let's go back to war and killing people so it will look good? All of these are terrible choices, of course they are. The Earth is a living organism. You cannot say we will continue in spite of the icecaps melting and the Earth shifting and then we will have a freeze. You cannot say we will just go on because that is not what is coming. That act of nature and this ill-devised plan that has been very successful for a long time are going to collide. Then we will have other civilizations getting into the picture.

What I have done with my beautiful people for a very long time in time, knowing they are still caterpillars, is I have asked them to prepare for this time. I gave you a long, long time to get sovereign, to build a hovel in a place that could withstand nature's rage, even the volcano in the backyard. Put up food while it is cheap, lots of it. Make sure you have clean water and stay away from water. Don't build in lowlands or by the sea or by rivers. Your storage place should be in a safe area, and get ready to rumble. And keep adding to it. Keep storing, keep adding. It didn't mean you had to be a very wealthy person. It only meant that you started twenty years ago and you continued. That is prudence. The great species in nature — ants, bees, insects, and animals — will always see a time of plenty and are always storing food. Why is that not seen or understood by you?

Many of my beautiful people who absolutely started that gave up because they said, "The

Days to Come are not coming. They are not here." Oh, yes, they are. Once I was a lone voice but now everyone is talking about it. It is beautiful. I am very pleased with that. Some of it is wrong but speculation, nonetheless. My people did what I asked and worked with that and were absolutely abused by everybody. Now it is the wisest thing anybody can do, and everyone is told they should do it. There was always a point in time that you had to do all of this work and in the meantime learn all about yourself so we could get to days like today. Without too much arguing for your limitations, you could actually and functionally stay tuned, pay attention, and indeed have a realization and be willing to start looking at yourself. That was not always possible before. Now we are prepared, and we get prepared up here in your brain from which all reality flows.

As Ramtha the Enlightened One, I already know that life continues. But if I tell that to this conservative group here, they will do nothing. Somehow you think you are really powerful, that you know it all, but you haven't wired that knowingness through the power of application. It is just stored information.

Somehow you feel that you don't have to do anything, and you don't. It is not required. It is just a voice of another time telling you that there are great kingdoms to come. You should live to see them, truly live to see them. In the process of downloading the future and indeed downloading the technologies, it allows your mind to be like a golden light that starts here, quickly disappears, and appears in a time frame in which the scene is completely different. It is ten years from now, twenty years from now. This golden light appears in this frame. That is your mind. It is planting the soil. You now have a line from that light, ten years, to this place. You have a destiny, and you have room to expand and grow.

When you are visiting and downloading the future, you should download access to new technology. You should put yourself in a winning position way out here with the people who are the creators, the generators of it. Make yourself frequency specific to them. It is not using them; it is being one of them. Start working on that. You may not know how to put anything together; you are not required to. The neurons that you have that are downloaded with all this genius will come into place and start to fire and you will meet people from the future-Now who will know how to do all of this, and you will be integral to it and will evolve to understand it. That is how you access improbable and impossible possibilities. It starts here with genuine and earnest focus. Start here on anything, but you have to nourish it. You cannot just say it. It can't just be your philosophy. It has to shine from you, supremely.

Closing Words:
Nature and Your Future Self

"I want you to work on the architecture of your new self. I want you, to whatever degree you wish to do that, to participate in your own redemption, indeed your own spiritual growth that enables you to be inwardly responsible, and then use it."
— *Ramtha*

At last then, from this material, I know that I have changed the hearts and minds of a few of you that would otherwise have never made it. I have my magic number one, two, three, four, five, six, seven, and on.

My beloved people, we started with hope and despair. We started working and found hope and jubilance. We now have hope and more hope. Until I meet you again, I want you to work on the architecture of your new self. I want you, to whatever degree you wish to do that, to participate in your own redemption, indeed your own spiritual growth that enables you to be inwardly responsible, and then use it. Work within its parameters, its program, long enough to get some wiring going in. It can always be modified, but start. And when you Create Your Day®, let the new architecture be the foundation of how you are going to create the day — not creating a day from lack — because you have already planted the bulb of wealth. You Create Your Day® according to that architecture of change, and all of you need to do that.

I would counsel you, as your teacher, that when you leave this bright, shining day and go to your hovels, find a place — a bush, a tree, a barren ground — that perhaps you know very well what is planted there. You know very well what your jasmine bush looks like or your rose bush. Sit and just look at the ground for a moment or the bush and just imagine how

large it is going to get this year, how many
more heady flowers will come out of it with
their fragrance and perfume. Just look at that
and don't talk to your gabby friends. Just say, "I
want my God to look at this. I want to see this
for the first time." Have a true talisman of your
own reality. How is it going to grow and how
is it going to be nourished? You will have such
sweet and beautiful hope spring from you. A
certitude will come, that what is in nature, so am
I. And I begin the work as the butterfly, indeed.

You do that as the great student of the Great
Work. You change your world. You cannot
change the world until you change. You can't
make happy what is not happy if you are not
happy. You are in the center of your reality. I
beseech you this day to earnestly look at nature
and learn sweetly from it. It is a bright morning,
and with that I say to you I have accomplished my
work with you this day. You and I did very well.

To the future.

— *Ramtha*

RAMTHA'S SELECTED GLOSSARY
OF TERMS AND DISCIPLINES

For more information on Ramtha's teachings, his disciplines and techniques for personal transformation and focus, please visit or write to Ramtha's School of Enlightenment, P.O. Box 1210, Yelm, WA 98597, U.S.A., www.ramtha. com. Ramtha's book, *A Beginner's Guide to Creating Reality,* Third Edition (JZK Publishing, 2004), contains Ramtha's introduction to his teachings, his disciplines, and his School of Enlightenment.

Analogical Mind: Being analogical means living in the Now. It is the creative moment and is outside of time, the past, and the emotions.

Bands, the: The bands are the two sets of seven frequencies that surround the human body and hold it together. Each of the seven frequency layers of each band corresponds to the seven seals of seven levels of consciousness in the human body. The bands are the auric field that allow the processes of binary and analogical mind.

Binary Mind: This term means two minds. It is the mind produced by accessing the knowledge of the human personality and the physical body without accessing our deep subconscious mind. Binary mind relies solely on the knowledge, perception, and thought processes of the neocortex and the first three seals. The fourth, fifth, sixth, and seventh seals remain closed in this state of mind.

Blue Body®: The body that belongs to the fourth plane of existence, the bridge consciousness, and the ultraviolet frequency band. The Blue Body® is the lord over the lightbody and the physical plane. It is also a discipline taught by Ramtha in which the students lift their conscious awareness to the consciousness of the fourth plane. This discipline allows the Blue Body® to be accessed and the fourth seal to be opened for the purpose of healing or changing the physical body. This technique is taught exclusively at Ramtha's School of Enlightenment.

Consciousness & Energy — C&E®: "The breath of power." Abbreviation of Consciousness & Energy®. This is the service mark of the fundamental discipline of manifestation and the raising of consciousness taught in Ramtha's School of Enlightenment. Through this discipline the students learn to create an analogical state of mind, open up their higher seals, and create reality from the

Void. A Beginning C&E® Workshop is the name of the introductory workshop for beginning students in which they learn the fundamental concepts and disciplines of Ramtha's teachings. The teachings of the Beginning C&E® Workshop can be found in *Ramtha, A Beginner's Guide to Creating Reality,* Third Ed. (Yelm: JZK Publishing, a division of JZK, Inc., 2004.) This technique is taught exclusively at Ramtha's School of Enlightenment.

Create Your Day®: Discipline created by Ramtha for raising consciousness and energy and intentionally creating a plan of events and experiences for the day very early in the morning before the activities of the day begin. This technique is taught exclusively at Ramtha's School of Enlightenment.

Fieldwork®: This is one of the fundamental disciplines of Ramtha's School of Enlightenment. The students are taught to create a symbol of something they want to know and experience and draw it on a paper card. These cards are placed with the blank side facing out on the fence rails of a large field. The students blindfold themselves and focus on their symbol, allowing their body to walk freely to find their card through the application of the law of consciousness and energy and analogical mind. This technique is taught exclusively at Ramtha's School of Enlightenment.

JZ Knight: JZ Knight is the only channel through whom Ramtha has chosen to deliver his message. Ramtha refers to JZ as his beloved daughter. She was Ramaya, the eldest of the children given to Ramtha during his lifetime.

List, the: The List is the discipline taught by Ramtha where the student gets to write a list of items they desire to know and experience and then learn to focus on it in an analogical state of consciousness. The List is the map used to design, change, and reprogram the neuronet of the person. It is the tool that helps to bring meaningful and lasting changes in the person and their reality. This technique is taught exclusively at Ramtha's School of Enlightenment.

Neighborhood Walk®: Discipline created by JZ Knight for raising consciousness and energy to intentionally modify our brain's neuronet and preestablished patterns of thinking that we no longer desire and to replace them with new ones of our own choice. This technique is taught exclusively at Ramtha's School of Enlightenment.

Sending-And-Receiving: Discipline created by Ramtha to develop the brain's innate ability for telepathy and remote-viewing, both with a specific target or a partner, anywhere, anything, or any time, past, present or future.

Tank®, The: It is the name given to the labyrinth used as part of the disciplines of Ramtha's School of Enlightenment. The students are taught to find the entry to this labyrinth blindfolded and move through it focusing on the Void without touching the walls or using the eyes or the senses. The objective of this discipline is to find, blindfolded, the center of the labyrinth or a room designated and representative of the Void.

Twilight®, Visualization Process: It is the process used to practice the discipline of the List or other visualization formats. The student learns to access the alpha state in the brain with focused intent in a state similar to deep sleep, yet retaining their conscious awareness.

Void, the: The Source. The Void is defined as one vast nothing materially, yet all things potentially.

ABOUT RAMTHA'S SCHOOL OF ENLIGHTENMENT

Ramtha's School of Enlightenment (RSE), created by Ramtha the Enlightened One, is an academy of the mind.

Using ancient wisdom and the latest discoveries in neuroscience and quantum physics, RSE offers retreats and workshops and teaches students of all ages and cultures how to access the extraordinary abilities of the brain to "Become a Remarkable Life®."

Ramtha is a legendary Master Teacher who mastered his own humanity centuries ago and returned in our modern times to tell his story and teach us what he learned. He explains that in his lifetime he addressed the questions about human existence and the meaning of life, and that through his own observation, reflection, and contemplation he became enlightened and conquered the physical world and death. His philosophy reflects the experience of his own life. Ramtha's teachings are not a religion. They offer a unique perspective from which to view the mystery of life.

237

Ramtha's teachings emphasize that each individual is responsible for their own reality, that your thoughts and attitudes affect and create your life, and that you can intentionally change your life by artfully changing your thought.

Ramtha communicates his wisdom by channeling through the body of JZ Knight. JZ Knight began publicly channeling Ramtha in 1979. RSE was established in 1988 in Yelm, Washington, and more than 100,000 people from around the world have attended Ramtha's events.

JZ Knight is the unique channel of Ramtha and author of the best-selling autobiography, *A State of Mind, My Story*. Historians and religious experts who have studied her life's work call JZ Knight the Great American Channel and recognize her as one of the most charismatic and compelling spiritual leaders of the modern age. JZ Knight is the only channel through whom Ramtha has chosen to deliver his message. She and Ramtha have inspired audiences worldwide for the last three decades, bridging ancient wisdom and the power of consciousness together with the latest discoveries in science.

The home campus sits on 80 acres of pastoral, lush grounds and towering evergreens in Yelm, Washington. Great cedar and fir trees grace the grounds, and a sense of timelessness prevails. Events are conducted in the Great Hall, which can accommodate up to 1,000 students. RSE facilitates live events in many languages at the Yelm campus, at venues around the world, and via Internet streaming through www.ramtha.com. For more information, please visit www.ramtha.com.

"What is the job of the Master Teacher?
To give extraordinary knowledge, enough to
make the human mind query questions that
are no longer mundane but venture into the
outrageous
and the unfathomable,
because when asking such questions,
we awaken the Spirit and we awaken
the true spiritual nature of ourself."

"You can do anything.
The key is focus."

"One day I will have turned out Christs
from this school
and the world will rejoice,
for this is the mission."
— Ramtha

PUBLISHING

Retracing the Footsteps of
Ancient Wisdom in Our History

P.O. Box 15232
Tumwater, Washington 98511, U.S.A.
Visit us online:
www.Hun-Nal-Ye.com

Made in the USA
Middletown, DE
26 November 2018